HIGHER EDUCATION
Incentives and Obstacles

COMMITTEE ON EQUALITY OF OPPORTUNITY
IN HIGHER EDUCATION*

Appointed by the American Council on Education

Lawrence E. Dennis, Vice-President for Academic Affairs, The Pennsylvania State University; *Chairman*

Lucile Allen, Consultant, Austin College

Ralph F. Berdie, Professor of Psychology and Director of Student Counseling Bureau, University of Minnesota

Horace Mann Bond, Dean, School of Education, Atlanta University

Paul G. Bulger, President, College of Education at Buffalo (New York)

Otto Klineberg, Professor of Psychology, Columbia University

Rexford G. Moon, Jr., Director of the College Scholarship Service, College Entrance Examination Board

Richard L. Plaut, President, National Scholarship Service and Fund for Negro Students

Sister Columba, S.N.D., Vice-President, Trinity College

Andrew C. Smith, S.J., President, Spring Hill College

Glen Stice, Research Associate, Educational Testing Service

Donald E. Super, Professor of Education, Teachers College, Columbia University

Clyde Vroman, Director of Admissions, University of Michigan

Wendell W. Wright, Professor of Education, Indiana University

Arthur S. Adams, President, American Council on Education; *ex officio*

* Membership at the time of the conference.

HIGHER EDUCATION

INCENTIVES AND OBSTACLES

A REPORT OF AN INVITATIONAL CONFERENCE ON
ENCOURAGING PERSONAL INCENTIVE FOR HIGHER
EDUCATION AMONG TALENTED BUT DISADVANTAGED
YOUTH, SPONSORED BY THE AMERICAN COUNCIL ON
EDUCATION, NOVEMBER 1–3, 1959

Edited by NICHOLAS C. BROWN

AMERICAN COUNCIL ON EDUCATION   •   *Washington, D.C.*

PRINTED IN THE UNITED STATES OF AMERICA

Foreword

WHEN HUMAN TALENT IS WASTED, EVERYONE IS DEPRIVED; WHEN it is rightly developed, everyone benefits. Thus, in the long run, the fortunes of the individual and society rise and fall together.

The American concept of equality of educational opportunity is a mixture of idealism and pragmatism. On the one hand, it reflects our national conviction that every individual deserves the chance to develop his full potential; on the other hand, it reflects our confidence that society benefits most when each person is free to seek self-fulfillment according to his natural interests and abilities.

These two beliefs are fundamentally congenial. Conflict arises only when national manpower needs tend to distort normal career choices or when individual aspirations are too low because of lack of opportunity or challenge.

The importance of this concept of equality of educational opportunity to Americans can be measured by the degree to which it has been realized in a relatively short period of time. No other nation has so generously provided educational opportunities for so many of its people. No other nation has so zealously guarded the right of its children to choose freely their life work. Yet, no other nation has shown more concern for its educational shortcomings, however understandable they might be in the light of its ambitious goals and heroic achievements.

Despite its success, American education must confront the consequences of its failures. It has been variously estimated that from 100,000 to 200,000 talented high school graduates fail to continue their education each year for lack of money or motivation. Probably as many children of equal ability drop out, discouraged and undiscovered, before high school graduation.

v

Many of these students come from environments in which their incentive for further education is never aroused. Although schools alone have not caused this problem and although schools alone cannot solve it, educators at all levels are in a strategic position to assume leadership in attacking it.

The Council's Committee on Equality of Opportunity in Higher Education has long been concerned with the loss of development of human talent resulting from lack of personal incentive. While much attention has been given to the financial barriers to higher education, too little attention has been given to the more subtle, but no less real, environmental obstacles that prevent able youngsters from continuing their studies. Accordingly, on November 1–3, 1959, the committee sponsored a Conference on Encouraging Personal Incentive for Higher Education among Talented but Disadvantaged Youth. This publication is a report of that conference.

The Council gratefully acknowledges its indebtedness to the conference participants who gave their thoughtful attention to this problem and who, in so doing, provided the basis for this report. The Council also expresses its gratitude to the Ford Foundation for the funds that made both the conference and the report possible.

ARTHUR S. ADAMS, *President*
American Council on Education

Preface

AMERICAN HIGHER EDUCATION HAS A MORAL RESPONSIBILITY TO find and encourage students of high promise whose aspirations are too low. In many respects, personal incentive is the most important of all prerequisites for higher education, for it has no effective substitute. Whereas able young people influenced toward higher education by favorable environments develop drives sufficient to overcome formidable obstacles, those not so fortunately influenced seldom understand opportunities that are theirs. What they do not understand they do not value; what they do not value they do not pursue.

In the interest of society and in justice to the individual, ways must be devised to bring these talented but disadvantaged youth much closer to their human potentialities. In recent years, shortages of educated persons have intensified the growth of programs designed to enable young men and women of superior ability to develop their full capacities through higher education. This burgeoning interest has stimulated an insistent demand for additional scholarships and loans to help able but financially distressed high school graduates.

More than financial aid, however, is required to foster the maximum self-realization of talented youth. Although a relatively small amount of money might enable a well-motivated student to go to college, a substantial salary might not persuade a qualified but "mal-motivated" student to go at all! Thus, even among superior students who could secure financial help, there continues to be a lamentable loss of talent because of the lack of personal incentive.

The full development of human resources requires, therefore, at least two things: On the one hand, the removal of financial obstacles that result in inequalities of educational opportunities;

on the other hand, the removal of environmental barriers that severely limit the horizons of some students as they seek to find their individual ways toward self-fulfillment.

The latter task calls for a better understanding on the part of parents, teachers, and counselors of how career attitudes are formed. Family indifference, negative community pressures, distorted social values, and the likelihood of postcollege socioeconomic restrictions can affect adversely a series of personal choices relating to one's educational future just as surely as can lack of money.

While it supports the efforts that are being made to remove economic barriers, the Council's Committee on Equality of Opportunity in Higher Education believes that a maximum effort must now be made to overcome other major impediments which tend to obscure the vision and obstruct the natural educational progress of many well qualified students. With this conviction, the committee seeks by means of this conference report to focus attention on effective ways (1) to encourage personal incentive for higher education among talented but disadvantaged youth, (2) to identify the forces that tend to stifle that incentive, and (3) to initiate action that will counteract such forces.

LAWRENCE E. DENNIS, *Chairman*
Committee on Equality of Opportunity
in Higher Education

Contents

List of Tables

Assessment of Current Trends
of Opportunity for Higher Education

ALGO D. HENDERSON

Director, Center for the Study of Higher Education, University
of Michigan; Former Chairman, Committee on Equality
of Opportunity in Higher Education

GLANCING AT THE HUGE ENROLLMENTS OF COLLEGES AND UNIVERSI-
ties, one might ask, "Is there any question about opportunity for
higher education in the United States?" We have more than
doubled the number of students who were in these institutions
during the years before World War II. We have several times
the number of students in our colleges than has any other country
in the world.

The fact that the question about opportunity is raised indicates
that we have a new point of view toward the role of higher education. Formerly, college was thought of as an experience that
should be available to those individuals who desired to attend
and who had the requisite qualifications for admission. As of
today, we have not lost sight of this view; however, we have developed two additional principles that serve as bases for the formation of policy. One, the nation should cultivate its human
resources. This means that all of the youth of given talent should
be sought out and encouraged to get additional education. Two,
this policy should be implemented by seeing to it, in positive
ways, that equal opportunity shall be given to persons irrespective
of their socioeconomic status or factors of race, color, creed, or
national origin. Analyses will show that whereas we have made
progress toward achieving these two goals, we are also deficient
in many respects in attaining them.

1

Financial Barriers

Superficially, it may appear that there is no financial problem facing the college student of today. Students in large numbers are attending college, which means that they are commanding the finances to do so. Some students have lots of money to spend— witness the thousands of student-owned automobiles. It might also be pointed out that there has been an impressive growth in the number of scholarships and the amount of loan funds available for the needy student.

Contradicting these superficial appearances are certain other facts. Sibley was able to demonstrate in New York State the high correlation between college attendance and the amount of family income.[1] Although there has been a difference of opinion as to whether the principal factor has been lack of motivation or lack of money, there has been little doubt that money is an important factor. It seems highly probable that lack of motivation for many grows out of environmental conditions which in turn reflect low family incomes.

In spite of our ongoing prosperity in the United States there are many families that include college-age children where the income is low. In 1958 half of the families of the United States had incomes below $5,050. Fourteen percent of them fell below $2,000, 22 percent were in the $2,000–$3,999 group and another 25 percent received between $4,000 and $5,999. For those families in the lower half, the sending of a boy or girl to a tuition-charging, residential college at a minimum cost of $1,200 to $1,-500 a year is difficult. Having two or three children in college at a time really squeezes the pocketbook. The problem mounts still more for the 36 percent of the families with incomes below $4,000.

Another fact of importance is that the trend of costs to the student has been rising. According to the U.S. Office of Education, tuition and fees in 1957 as compared with 1940, the last prewar year, were higher by 89 percent in public colleges and 83 percent in private ones.[2] During the same seventeen-year period,

[1] Elbridge Sibley, "The Relation Between College Attendance and Economic Status," *Matching Needs and Facilities in Higher Education*, New York Legislative Document (1948), No. 31, p. 116.

[2] Ernest V. Hollis and Associates, *Costs of Attending College*, U.S. Office of Education Bulletin 1957, No. 9 (Washington: Government Printing Office, 1957), p. 29.

the Bureau of Labor Statistics cost-of-living index increased from 59.5 to 117.8, or 98 percent. Thus, the increase in fees appears merely to have kept pace with the changing value of the dollar. For private institutions this may be necessary and justified. For public ones, continued increases in charges create an ever-widening departure from the principle of free public instruction. Or if one were to grant the political necessity for public institutions to assess part of the operating cost against the students, it must be recognized that the mounting cost militates against, rather than works toward, providing better opportunity for the boys and girls from lower-income families.

The increases in charges at individual institutions have, of course, varied widely. A recent study [3] of 53 private colleges in New York State and 46 state universities shows increases over the last seven years ranging from 5 to 68 percent. The basic college expenses (tuition and fees, and, in residential colleges, room and board) of undergraduate students in the 99 institutions reporting, are shown in Table 1.

TABLE 1.—BASIC COLLEGE EXPENSES PER YEAR REPORTED BY 99 INSTITUTIONS, SHOWING INCREASES OVER SEVEN-YEAR PERIOD, 1953–59

TYPE OF INSTITUTION	EXPENSES		PERCENT OF INCREASE
	1953–54	1959–60	
43 private residential colleges in New York:			
Median	$1,425	$1,885	28
Range	$915–$2,466	$1,207–$2,830	8–51
10 private nonresidential colleges in New York:			
Median	$558	$793	52
Range	$427–$725	$575–$1,100	15–68
46 state universities:			
Median	$733	$898	21
Range	$504–$1,055	$675–$1,170	5–61

All institutions, both public and private, are finding it difficult to secure sufficient funds for their operating and capital construction budgets. This has put pressures on these institutions to

[3] University of the State of New York, *Department Fact Sheet*, No. 2, 1959–60 series (September 1959).

raise the tuition charges. The increases that have been made thus far are modest in comparison with those that are being advocated in some quarters. Seymour Harris, for example, has proposed that the public colleges and universities should adjust their charges to cover 40 percent of the operating costs (a jump of 100 percent) and the private institutions should make charges that approximately cover the operating costs.[4] He believes that if students were granted credit which would enable them to pay these bills over a long period of years, they would find it quite feasible to do so. In my judgment, the Harris type of proposal is reactionary in that it would contravene the progress made during the past century in recognizing the public interest in educating the young people of America.

Of similar nature are other practices and proposals that tend to force students to pay for the costs of buildings. The movement to have students finance dormitories by amortizing loans has become accepted practice. In a typical plan of this sort, the room rents include a 20 percent loading to provide funds from which interest and annual payments are made on the loan. This plan has been working well and many dormitories have been erected which otherwise might not have been built. I think there is reasonable justification for charging the true cost of room and board including the cost of facilities to the student. In doing so, however, we must recognize that we are adding to the financial burdens of students who do not have good incomes.

Bills have been introduced in certain of the legislatures calling for the floating of bond issues for the purpose of erecting classroom buildings and providing for the bonds to be retired from special fees levied on the students. Although such legislation has not as yet been passed, legislators who are under pressure to hold the line on taxes may become tempted with the plan. Unless the colleges and universities remain constantly alert to the dangers in this kind of move, we may find that the policy of providing educational plants through public and philanthropic funds has been modified or abandoned.

[4] Seymour E. Harris, "College Salaries, Financing of Higher Education, and Management of Institutions of Higher Learning," *AAUP Bulletin*, XLIV (September 1958), 589–95.

Where colleges are located near the homes of the students, additional opportunity for attendance is created. Evidence on this point may be found in the report of the Michigan Legislative Study Committee on Higher Education.[5] Relative to the college-age group, the average percentages of attendance at college in various types of counties were found to be the following: counties having no college, 16.9; counties having only a private college, 27.5; counties having a public community college, 32.1; counties having a state college, 39.6. In Michigan, the fees at all public colleges are modest, and commuting is a common practice. It seems clear that a public institution which has no fees or only low fees and which is so located as to enable students to live at home can supply the needs of students at a very low annual cost. To some extent, private institutions can do so. Students attending such institutions can, if need be, work their way. College becomes possible for the children of families of low income if the family can give a small amount of help, such as providing the room and board of the student.

In the above analysis, I have had principally in mind the undergraduate student. At the graduate and advanced professional levels, we have a much more serious situation. Able students from low-income families may want to go beyond the bachelor's degree. If they have the requisite ability, it is strongly in the interests of the nation to have them do so. However, most students beyond twenty-one years of age are apt to marry and, in many cases, have children. At this age and under these circumstances, the student may question whether he should expect additional help from home. In any event, his annual budget may have doubled or quadrupled. At the same time, he is foregoing the opportunity to earn a salary during these years, although he often works part time. This is a problem for the nation as well as for the individual because it is from among these students that come the future college teachers, scientists, physicians, and other professional men and creative leaders.

As noted earlier, one of the proposals for providing opportunity is to make loans to students. This appears to be an underlying

[5] Michigan Legislative Study Committee on Higher Education, *Preliminary Report*, March 1957, pp. 57–58.

philosophy of the National Defense Education Act of 1958. Congress made certain provision for loans to students and some provision for graduate fellowships, but eliminated from the bill the proposal for scholarships. The National Defense Education Act is a definite step forward. It is an additional recognition on the part of our Federal Government of partial responsibility for the financing of some aspects of higher education. It is a recognition of some responsibility to extend financial aid to college students in encouraging the development of our human resources. The loan program has been reasonably successful, partly because the funds available at any one institution are small. It has especially appealed to students who are aiming toward teaching careers and thus have a prospect of having 50 percent of the loan canceled.

The idea of student loans is enticing. We borrow money with which to build homes, buy automobiles, and install television sets. Why should not families do the same in helping their children to become educated? If banks and insurance companies can make loans successfully for the purchase of goods, could they not do so with equal success in making loans to young people who have promising careers ahead? In view of anticipated increased income during his lifetime as a result of his study, could not the student well afford to borrow money in order to secure the necessary training?

Although loan funds may help selected individuals, I am personally dubious about them as any general solution to the problem of finances. At institutions where there have been substantial loan funds, they have not been fully used. For a variety of reasons, students hesitate to encumber themselves with substantial loans that need to be paid off in the future. They may hesitate to launch upon a career with this type of obligation hanging over them. Having incurred this debt, they may find it difficult to borrow additional funds needed to set up an office or in other ways get launched on some enterprise or occupation of their own. Students who anticipate going into low-paid careers, as in the ministry, in social service, in teaching, and in many phases of public service, can ill afford to obligate themselves for annual payments on loans. Women students may be especially hesitant to undertake obligations which later might have to be assumed by their husbands.

From the social point of view, there should not be pressure upon the student to select a high-paying occupation in order to make it easier to pay off an obligation. Finally, the assumption that underlies the loan plan, namely, that the student should pay a large part of the cost of his education, is contrary to the needs in society today. Such a policy would impede the attendance of students at college rather than encourage attendance. It would penalize students from lower-income families because these persons would begin their careers with substantial debt whereas other students would not.

It will easily be discerned that I strongly favor stemming the tide of rising costs to the students and doing anything we can to reverse it. I feel strongly that such action would be in accord with the American principle of opportunity. It would be in accord with our concept of free public education, including higher education, which was implied in the wording of the Northwest Ordinance. It would be consistent with the reasoning of the Supreme Court of Michigan in the 1872 Kalamazoo case which decided once and for all that it was appropriate and legitimate to use public funds to establish free high schools. It would be in accord with the constitutions of the several states that prohibit the public institutions from charging tuition.

In view of the public concern about the progress being made in Soviet Russia in the education of technicians, engineers, and scientific personnel, we need to consider seriously the trends of increasing costs to the students in the United States. Inasmuch as Soviet Russia provides free higher education and indeed provides the student with money to cover additional living costs, may we not fall seriously behind her in our search for talent if we do not keep education low in cost to the student? Far from emulating Soviet Russia, this would merely be a return to our earlier and traditional policy.

Lest I leave too gloomy a picture about the financial barriers to the education of youth, I should like to summarize a few encouraging trends:

1. As noted earlier, the National Defense Education Act of 1958 represents the enunciation of a new policy by our Federal Government and is an encouraging step in a new direction.

2. A number of new scholarship programs have been launched in recent years and the total sums available for student scholarships have been substantially increased. The programs are too numerous to give in detail but mention should be made of those established by various corporations, of the scholarships of the National Merit Scholarship Foundation, of the enlargements that have been made in several state scholarship programs including New York, California, and Illinois, and of the generous fellowships being given by the National Science Foundation.

3. The actions of the American Association of Land-Grant Colleges and State Universities and the State Universities Association in opposing proposals which would cause students to pay more of the cost of their education, and in publicizing the dangers inherent in such proposals, deserve commendation.

4. The public community college movement is growing rapidly. Being free or low in cost, and serving students who continue to live at home, this type of college is a most promising development toward the removal of economic barriers. Regionally placed public four-year colleges and universities make similar contributions.

Geographic Barriers

A portion of what has already been said relating to financial barriers to opportunity applies also to geographic barriers. However, certain trends that are resulting in the decentralized location of institutions of higher education should be noted. We also need to be aware of some dangers that lie ahead.

One of the trends is in the increase in public two-year colleges. The number has grown to about 400, with a gross enrollment of approximately 800,000. The students include 13 percent of the total regular college enrollment; also older persons who have returned to college for special purposes.

The reports of the two Presidential commissions on higher education and all of the state surveys give prominent attention to the potentialities in the public community college for serving large numbers of students. Ordinarily these institutions offer at least two types of programs—college parallel and terminal-occupational. Ordinarily they admit students on the basis of a high school diploma. As public institutions, they charge low tuitions and in some states, as in California, are free. Their programs meet the needs of some students who would not be eligible for admission to other colleges or whose interests lie in occupational fields where two years of college training suffice.

Thus these institutions are providing opportunity to students near their homes where the cost of living is largely cared for in the home. In California, the public junior colleges now enroll approximately 70 percent of the freshmen and sophomores who are in public higher institutions in the state. This extraordinary demonstration in one state is suggestive of what may happen in many states.

Another movement that is bringing additional opportunity on a regional or state basis is the transformation of the state teachers colleges into multiple-unit colleges or universities. This trend is now well advanced, a substantial portion of the states having already made the conversion. The reorganized state college typically introduces two or more additional programs—liberal arts, business administration, and master's degree work in teacher education. A considerable number of the colleges have become universities with still additional curricula. Some states, such as California, have increased the number of these institutions, placing the new ones in regions that previously did not have a state college. These institutions are bringing general education and vocational and professional courses within reach of hundreds of thousands of additional students. Somewhat parallel with this movement has been the establishment by some state colleges and universities of additional centers or off-campus college units. Still other states, such as Florida, are launching new regional universities.

New institutions are also being founded by private groups or organizations. The Catholic Church has been active in establishing new colleges, in adding upper-class programs to junior colleges, and, in a few instances, in inviting lay students to attend colleges that previously had been restricted to the religious. Another interesting development has been the broadening of the programs of a number of Bible schools to include degree curricula in liberal arts. A few independent colleges have also been established. Coupled with these movements has been one to strengthen and enlarge private colleges that have not achieved accreditation by a regional association.

It may be recalled that during the postwar years when there was a large influx of students into the colleges and universities, the institutions began to erect barriers against certain types of students and some states established quotas that barred many out-of-state students. These restrictions have been noticeably relaxed. However, we have about reached the stage when fresh pressures will be felt because of the much higher birth rate that occurred following 1940. It seems only realistic to anticipate that these pressures may again cause barriers of these types to be adopted.

Segregation and Discriminations

Additional barriers to opportunity in higher education occur because of institutional or state policies for the segregation of Negro and non-Negro students and because of discrimination against minority groups. In discussing briefly the subject of segregation, I shall confine my remarks to the practices in higher education. It should be apparent, however, that the segregation of Negro children in schools that are below the standards of those provided for white students limits the graduates of these schools in preparing themselves for admission to, and carrying successfully educational work at, the college level. To some extent, the resulting environmental influences may also cause able young Negroes to fail to consider or to reject further study in college.

Assuming as I do that segregation in any form is an outmoded social pattern, the principal effect of the decision of the United States Supreme Court in 1954 which declared segregation to be illegal was to remove from the social custom its legal support.[6] There can no longer be any question as to the illegality of these

---

[6] Brown *et al.* v. Board of Education of Topeka, Shawnee County, *et al.*, 347 U.S. 483.

practices. In spite of regional attitudes, there can no longer be any question that national policy is opposed to segregation.

While the significance of the 1954 decision is thus recognized, we should not overlook the fact that in the case of higher education this decision had been preceded by a series of decisions that brought pressures upon the states to eliminate practices of segregation. I refer specifically to the Murray, Gaines, Sipuel, McLaurin, and Sweatt cases.[7] The import of these cases was that the Supreme Court was insisting that the provision of higher education for Negro students must be fully equal to that provided for the whites. Because the numbers of Negro students were few and the costs of constructing plant and operating programs were large, several of the states that had practiced segregation began to admit Negro students to the previously all-white graduate and professional schools and, in some instances, to undergraduate programs. Thus, as of 1954, twelve of the seventeen states that had practiced segregation had admitted one or more Negroes to public colleges or universities. Since 1954, one additional state has done so and now there remain only Mississippi, Alabama, Georgia, and South Carolina which as yet have refused.

The decision in the Brown case has caused the individuals opposed to integration to consolidate their forces and to make attempts to arouse public opinion against desegregation. At the college level, this reactionary movement has doubtless had some impact on many colleges and universities. On the other hand, the decision appears to have brought support to many institutions where the faculties and administration were merely conforming to local practices against their better judgments. The legal prop having been removed, such faculty groups have had a greater measure of freedom in moving cautiously forward.

In several of the border states, the colleges have become completely desegregated. According to Guy Johnson, of the 553 formerly all-white colleges and universities in seventeen states and the District of Columbia, 252, or 45 percent, have been desegre-

[7] See Algo D. Henderson, "Current Status of Equality of Opportunity in Higher Education," *Approaching Equality of Opportunity in Higher Education* (Washington: American Council on Education, 1955), pp. 14–26.

gated in practice or in principle.[8]   Thirteen of the thirty-five formerly all-Negro institutions have also been desegregated.[9]

When the institutions were subdivided by types of sponsorship, Johnson showed the percentages that have been desegregated to be as follows: public, 57 percent; private, 28 percent; Protestant, 33 percent; Roman Catholic, 88 percent.   The poor records of the private and the Protestant colleges are deplorable.   The Catholic institutions, in sharp contrast, have been showing leadership consistent with Christian principles.

A glance at local scenes provides further evidence of the breakdown of segregation.   In Texas, twenty-eight of the state's fifty-one public colleges and twenty-five of its private and church-related colleges have been desegregated.   Kentucky wiped out its segregation law, as a result of which all of the eight state-supported institutions quickly moved to admit Negroes.   West Virginia State College, formerly a Negro land-grant college, now has about as many white as Negro students.   Louisiana State University in New Orleans opened in the fall of 1959 with 417 Negroes among its 2,200 students.[10]

To the best of my knowledge, the integration in these many institutions has been effected without serious incident.   As an example, Memphis State University this fall admitted Negroes for the first time.   According to the newspaper report, there was no incident or disturbance.

Still other facts help to round out the picture of the improving opportunity for Negroes.   As of 1958, the number of Negroes in the United States that possessed earned doctorates was 673, most of them from distinguished universities.[11]   At its January 1958 convention, the Association of American Law Schools voted to censure member schools that refused to admit qualified Negroes.   In 1957, the Southern Association of Colleges and Secondary Schools admitted eighteen Negro colleges to full membership for the first

[8] Guy B. Johnson, "Desegregation and the Future of the Negro College: A Critical Summary," *Journal of Negro Education*, XXVII (Summer 1958), 430–35.

[9] "Status of School Segregation-Desegregation in the Southern and Border States" (Nashville, Tenn.: Southern Educational Reporting Service, Sixth Printing, May 15, 1959).

[10] *Southern School News*, VI (October 1959), 1.

[11] Johnson, *op. cit.*, p. 456.

time and took action to eliminate by 1961 its segregated list.[12] From facts such as the above, I think that only one conclusion can be drawn, that segregation of Negroes at the college level is on its way out.

Discriminatory practices among the colleges and universities seem also to have diminished materially since the close of World War II. It may be recalled that during the period of congested conditions that followed the war, the evidence of discrimination in admissions to college and to certain professional schools, notably medicine, was quite strong. It soon became evident that the American people were not indifferent to such practices. Such investigations as those by the city council in New York City and by the legislative commission in New York State were in response to these public pressures. As a result, institutions modified their practices and at least three of the states passed legislation making discrimination in certain types of cases illegal. Two restudies that were made in New York and Connecticut after some lapses of time indicated that discriminations had been substantially reduced.

Discriminations heretofore practiced against Negro students in Northern and Western institutions have materially diminished. It has now become unlikely that there would be any flagrant instance of discrimination on a Northern college campus without the act being vigorously condemned by faculty and students. The student governments have been especially alert to these events.

The resistance to the elimination of discriminatory practices now focuses principally in the fraternities and sororities. Even here some progress has been made because many of these fraternal organizations have eliminated the bias clauses in their constitutions. A number of colleges and universities have given notice to the fraternities that the clauses must be removed within a stated period of years if the group is to continue to be recognized by the institution. Ordinarily the difficulty is not with the local chapter of students but with the national organization, which is dominated by alumni.

I assume that the concept of fraternal life held by these alumni

[12] *Quarterly Review of Higher Education Among Negroes,* XXVI (January 1958), 103.

is that of social assimilation on a restricted basis that results in a brotherhood among the members of all chapters and alumni groups around the nation. What is patently needed is new leadership with a fresh viewpoint about the values in fraternity life. Now that the chapter houses resemble small hotels and the national membership comprises a small army, it becomes a bit ridiculous to assume the existence of brotherly affection among the members of all of the chapters on a national scale. If the fraternity continues to have valid reasons for existing, aside from providing dormitory space, these must lie in the educative value of group experiences, of creating situations where leadership may emerge, of having laboratories where interpersonal and intercultural understandings may be developed, and of having focal centers for the development of over-all loyalties to the college and to the principles underlying the good life. If such objectives could become the *raison d'être* for having fraternities, the institutions might be worth maintaining and encouraging. Otherwise, the universities would do well to drop them, as the State University of New York did in 1953.

The battle against discrimination is by no means over. Prejudices exist in nearly every community, and they affect the lives of students in many ways, such as in getting haircuts, renting apartments, and gathering at social events.

A final type of discrimination may exist in subtle ways that reduces opportunity for women. For example, although a medical school or an engineering school may be open to women, it may not be congenial toward them. In this case, the women meet a barrier. In the high schools, the girls equal the boys in numbers and abilities and outrank them in achievement. But beyond the high school, the number of women drops to about half the men. Here is an insufficiently tapped reservoir of talent. The doors to the professions and occupations should be opened wider for women.

Conclusion

Comparing the report in this paper with a similar one that I made before a conference called by this committee in 1954, I feel that definite progress in providing better opportunity has been made during the five years on several fronts. Segregation in higher education is on its way out, the legal props having been knocked from under it. Discriminations on grounds of race, creed, color, and national origin appear to be fewer in number and less flagrant as cases.

The interest of the Federal Government, which had performed such a notable service to veterans through the GI scholarships, has been rekindled through a generous program of fellowships provided by the National Science Foundation and the program of fellowships and loans under the National Defense Education Act of 1958. The latter act may well be the beginning of the acceptance of additional responsibility by the government. Scholarship programs have been augmented materially by the contributions of corporations and by the plan of the National Merit Scholarship Corporation.

The community college movement continues to expand both in numbers of institutions and in total enrollments. Many state colleges that formerly served a single purpose, such as for teacher education, have become multipurpose institutions. Some new colleges and universities have been founded and other universities have established additional off-campus centers and college units. In various of these ways, additional opportunity has been created for students and especially for those students who for financial or other reasons need to attend college near their homes.

Perhaps it should be noted also that the general prosperity of the country has undoubtedly helped make it possible for additional students and their families to provide the finances with which to attend college.

The scene is not wholly rosy, however. The costs of education have been steadily increasing both for the student and for the institutions. Tuition and fees and charges for room and board have all been advancing. This may not be a handicap for some students, but it increases the financial problem for students from the lower socioeconomic groups. Proposals have been advanced to increase the student charges still further as a means of helping to finance increases in faculty salaries and a larger scale of operations. Such proposals are contrary to the American traditions relating to public education and conflict sharply with the public interest in developing our human resources.

Discriminatory practices still lurk in the shadows, and segregation continues as a dark stain on the national character and as our most baffling internal problem.

The larger birth rate subsequent to 1940 is beginning to cause a considerable swelling in the enrollments of the colleges and universities. Assuming that history may repeat itself, we should be alert to the possibility that states may erect barriers against out-of-state students and that institutions will reintroduce subtle forms of discrimination.

Although we at this conference may take much satisfaction in the developments of the past five years, we should nevertheless prepare to defend the advances that have been made and move forward toward the goal of full opportunity to all American youth.

Our Larger Purposes

JOHN G. DARLEY

Executive Secretary, American Psychological Association

IT SEEMS STRANGE THAT, IN A SOCIETY WITH HIGHER PROPORTIONS OF youth in school than any other modern society, we should convene to study the problem embodied in the title of this conference. A reason may be found in a quotation from the *1959 Annual Report of the Carnegie Corporation.* There Dr. John Gardner said: "Most Americans honor education; few understand its larger purposes."

A reason may also be found in Gunnar Myrdal's book, *An American Dilemma:*[1] there is a dysfunction between the American creed and the American reality. As an outsider and a special observer, Myrdal wrote mainly of the American Negro problem, but he wrote of more than that when he pointed out the fundamental dysfunction that exists in many aspects of life between the American creed, to which we pay lip service, and the American reality, in which we allow inequities and inequalities to exist.

My thesis is that higher education itself has not adequately fulfilled its larger purposes and that some of its own spokesmen do not clearly enough understand them. I refer to the faculties and administrators of the 1,800 or more institutions of higher education in the United States.

Let me cite some evidence which seems to me to bear on the problem. This evidence will not be new to many of you in the audience who have pioneered in the collection of material of this kind; it is drawn from the nation-wide study of diversification in higher education under the direction of Dr. T. R. McCon-

[1] New York: Harper & Bros., 1944.

17

nell at the University of California at Berkeley, where it has been my good fortune since 1956 to serve as a consultant.

First of all, however, I want to recall for you two statements that have been made about the goals of higher education in the United States: one by the Commission on Higher Education appointed by President Truman, the other by the Commission on the Financing of Higher Education. The Truman Commission believed that the top 49 percent in ability of the age cohort should go on to grades thirteen and fourteen and that the top third to the top 38 percent should go on as far as they can in higher education. Speaking from a different philosophy, the Commission on Financing Higher Education stated that the task of higher education is to educate the top quarter of the age cohort through four or more years of college. These are hortatory statements about the goals of higher education; they are not alone derived from particular data; they are merely expressions of different points of view.

Now let us look briefly at some of the data regarding enrollment in higher education. In Dr. McConnell's study, we have been trying to do longitudinal studies of college students in states where the structure of higher education may be markedly different. In two states, Minnesota and Wisconsin, that are neither the best nor the poorest in their support of higher education, we followed a substantial sample of the September 1952 entering class in nearly all institutions.

In Minnesota, 44 percent of the male college entrants were drawn from the top quarter of their high school classes, and 31 percent were drawn from the bottom half of their high school classes. I have used these brackets, the top quarter and the bottom half, because they fit precisely the statements of the Truman Commission on Higher Education and the Commission on Financing Higher Education. Among women, 49 percent who entered colleges in Minnesota in 1952 came from the top quarter, and 22 percent came from the bottom half of their high school classes. Comparable figures from Wisconsin, collected by Dr. L. E. Drake in connection with Dr. McConnell's study, indicate that 32 percent of the men and 58 percent of the women were drawn from the top quarter. From the bottom half, 37 percent of the men and 16 percent of the women entered college.

Next, let us look at the survival rate in higher education without regard to ability at entrance. We have data on this from three states in Dr. McConnell's study. In Minnesota, our sample contained more than 90 percent of the students who entered colleges in the state; in Wisconsin, 70 percent; and in Ohio, slightly over 40 percent. By 1956–57, 44 percent of the men and 46 percent of the women who entered in Minnesota had graduated. In Wisconsin, 38 percent of the men and 42 percent of the women who entered had graduated. In Ohio, 48 percent of the men and 46 percent of the women had graduated. In short, *less than half* the entrants in each state had graduated over four years later!

In spite of the fact that less than 15 percent of either the men or the women had actually failed, 46 percent of the men and 48 percent of the women in Minnesota, 43 percent of the men and 49 percent of the women in Wisconsin, and 37 percent of the men and 47 percent of the women in Ohio had withdrawn before completing four years of higher education! The fact that surprised us was that quite often the students who withdrew in these states were not only approximately equal in ability to those who graduated but also had C averages or better when they withdrew. In each state, more women withdrew than men.

Let us look more closely at the superior students. In Minnesota, we identified students who were in the top quarter of their high school classes, as well as in the top quarter of ability according to the results of standardized tests. Among these high-potential students, 63 percent of the men graduated, and 37 percent withdrew or failed; 60 percent of the women graduated and 40 percent withdrew or failed.

These high-ability students entered the state colleges, the private colleges, and the state university in significantly different proportions, and they survived at different rates. Only 47 percent of the men of this high-potential group who went to the state colleges survived to graduation whereas 66 percent of the high-potential men who entered the university's liberal arts college and 73 percent who entered the several private colleges survived to graduation. Although similar percentages existed for high-potential students in Ohio and Wisconsin, time does not permit me to go into detail. The tragedy here is that we in higher education have been grossly negligent of our own competent students. It seems to me that we have disregarded the larger purposes of higher education by the casual way in which we have dealt with our best students. We simply have not discharged our responsibilities.

If these conditions obtain at the college level, where we are relatively well paid as faculty members, where we pride ourselves on our freedom, and where we think we know what we are doing, how much worse must the situation be in the high schools where the teachers are underpaid and where they are at the constant beck and call of the communities that treat them sometimes as mere servants.

These are not new facts. Dael Wolfle first pointed out in his book *America's Resources of Specialized Talent,*[2] that we were losing approximately 40 percent from the top quarter of our high school classes. The present figures from Minnesota and Wisconsin merely pinpoint with slightly greater precision Dr. Wolfle's findings. Dr. Iffert, who is attending this conference, earlier pointed out the differential holding power of various types of institutions. Although he did not closely relate it to ability levels, he made it perfectly clear that a great deal of ability was being lost in higher education through dropouts. Ralph F. Berdie and his colleagues at Minnesota have shown in the volume, *After High School—What?,*[3] the relation of ability to differential entry rates and have followed up the college-going plans of students in different segments of the ability range. Dr. Donald Super is doing a major study of vocational choices and interests as these relate to incentive for higher education.

The facts I have cited, then, are not essentially new; yet few of them seem to have had any real impact on educators. Byron Hollinshead, writing for the Commission on Financing Higher Education, gave some very cogent evidence showing which people

[2] New York: Harper & Bros., 1954.
[3] Minneapolis: University of Minnesota Press, 1954.

go to college and which do not.[4] A. B. Hollingshead, in *Elmtown's Youth*,[5] convincingly demonstrated the relationship of social class to educational and vocational planning. Dr. Stalnaker and his research staff at the National Merit Scholarship Corporation have discovered a great deal about incentive and college choice among bright students.[6] Pace and Stern have learned something about the "climates" of institutions as these relate to student needs and expectations.[7] Why do these findings remain so little used?

In some instances, higher education involves a dog-eat-dog competition among institutions for students. Consider the effect, for example, of excessive vocational emphasis as a method of getting enrollment. After calling attention to their virtues as private institutions of the liberal tradition, some colleges tell their prospective students how they can get vocational training by coming there. We have refused to recognize qualitative and type differences in higher education. Moreover, we maintain approximately 1,800 institutions, over half of which have enrollments of 500 students or less. I suggest it is physically impossible to maintain a decent quality of higher education in today's burgeoning fields of knowledge in institutions of that small size.

We have maintained a myth concerning public and private higher education, assuming that virtue resides in private higher education but not in public higher education. We have cherished the myth that there is something good in smallness and something evil in bigness. Can we continue to preserve this mythology as larger proportions of enrollments move toward public education? As public enrollments grow, public resources follow. The strong private institutions will not suffer, but, at the same time, the public institutions will become stronger as the enrollment tide rises in higher education. I predict that it will be the second- and third-rate private colleges that will suffer in the competition of the future.

[4] *Who Should Go to College?* (New York: Columbia University Press, 1954).
[5] New York: John Wiley & Sons, 1949.
[6] For some interesting data, see pp. 123–35.
[7] C. R. Pace and G. G. Stern, "Approach to the Measurement of Psychological Characteristics of College Environments," *Journal of Educational Psychology*, XLIX (October 1958), 269–77.

We have also preserved a myth about transferability among institutions. We say that students may start in the junior college or the community college and move on in large numbers to the four-year colleges and professional schools. The evidence on transfers, however, does not indicate that the junior college is a broad highway to educational heaven. In the Minnesota study only 624, or less than 20 percent, of the students who entered such in September 1952 later transferred to the state university within the four years of our follow-up. Those who transferred, of course, did well. Although we have told the public that local colleges are the beginning of the broad highway to full professional training, the figures on the volume of student transfer show this highway to be narrow and tortuous.

We have also in higher education today a very clear division of our forces between the democratic and aristocratic traditions. From the point of view of the aristocratic tradition, the oncoming hordes of students are genetic barbarians. From the point of view of the democratic tradition, as expressed in 1862 in the Morrill Act, we are engaged in a great movement to educate the children of all the people. The state universities and the land-grant institutions have brought us a long way toward the realization of this ideal, but we still have a long way to go. The conflict is not resolved.

About 40 percent of our present faculty members have the Ph.D., and, in the years ahead, this figure may fall to 20 percent. It is worth noting, however, that during the past two decades thirty graduate schools have produced 75 percent of all Ph.D.'s. The graduate students of these institutions have carried into their new positions their own image of what an institution should be. Their experience and convictions will exert real force in the democratic versus aristocratic struggle that continues in higher education.

Can we streamline higher education in any way? Is educational television a solution to at least some of our problems? Can we really change the most intransigent of all educational structures, the curriculum? Can we really change it so that it will make more sense in a modern society? Or will the curriculum continue to be the result of a balance of power forces, with each department striving to capture more enrollment—and money?

Can we learn more about the cause-effect and means-ends relations in higher education? At present, we do not know the processes by which we produce the miracles that we all think we are producing, and we get into terrific arguments over reforms in higher education. Nor do we know why we fail. I know of no major institution that maintains exit interviews in an attempt to hold the really good students who are withdrawing. I know women get married and drop out of school, but why do the men—especially the single men—withdraw when they are in good standing? How about the high-ability students that we let get away from us? We have no clear contact in higher education with the parents, except a proselyting type of contact when we promise them the world. We countenance no consumer's guide to higher education; yet, we make invidious comparisons happily in our own circles. We have a take-it-or-leave-it attitude about our students, in spite of advances made in the field of personnel work. We tolerate poor teaching and examining methods in higher education, although we would not, I think, allow them in secondary schools under the present system of supervision of teachers.

To mix quotations and sources: "Sweet are the uses of diversity in higher education, for they permit us to feel that all institutions are equal, although we admit that some are more equal than others." What are some of the possible solutions to our problems in higher education? Some forms of federal intervention? I think we can predict confidently that there will be more of these. We seldom question the interesting notion in this country that there is something sacred about local control. Education is no longer in the business of serving only the community. Education is in the business of serving a nation desperately needing help. The sanctity of local control has permitted some extremely bad and inadequate education to exist at all levels. Local control is often the barrier behind which some forces operate to keep the enterprise from being improved.

Education deals with our most precious natural resources: brain power, character, personality, and idealism. While I am not arguing for a removal of local control, I am arguing for the extension of local and federal partnership that is implicit in the Land-Grant Act, the National Science Foundation program, and the National Defense Education Act. No major university today, private or public, could do its job without the federal funds it receives for grants-in-aid, research contracts, and fellowship or training grants of one kind or another.

There are also private programs that help us solve our problems of conserving and developing human resources on a national scale. The Woodrow Wilson Fellowship program and the National Merit Scholarship program are good examples. I think we have come to recognize, however, that money alone is not going to provide the full solution. Although no one would doubt the power of money to bring about some correction of inequality, everyone must realize that the use of this money must be guided by an enlightened public philosophy.

If we attempt to restrict enrollments in the years ahead, I fear we are going to be proven entirely wrong. If an individual child strongly desires to go on to higher education, he and his parents will find a way. If a particular institution severely restricts its admissions, the student will go somewhere else. But he *will* go on to higher education. The present enrollment in higher education represents less than half of the age cohorts eligible for higher education. This enrollment has been showing increases of about 1 percent per year, over and above normal population growth, for a long time. More students are going to want higher education, and more parents are going to try to get it for them. The consumer will demand higher education, and he will get it because higher education, as well as secondary education, is at the service of the community that supports it. So we shall not solve the problem by changing admission requirements.

Another way to solve some of our problems is to make careful studies, institution by institution, of what we are doing and what our objectives truly are. We should really decide what we as a whole are trying to do and what each type of institution will try to do. We need far more research than we now have on how changes in behavior are brought about in the college years and even in the years prior to college when the choice about higher education is being made.

We must continuously study the problem of how to kindle talent of all kinds. We must improve our procedures so that it cannot be said that we have allowed 40 percent of our able students to drift away from our institutions without really understanding why they left and wherein we may have failed.

Our behavior must reflect our belief if our conduct is to match our creed. If we believe with John Gardner that education is "the servant of all our purposes," we shall labor to develop every human talent and help each child toward self-discovery and personal fulfillment. When we do this, our performance will be worthy of our larger purposes.

Discussion Following Dr. Darley's Address

Presiding: LAWRENCE E. DENNIS

LAWRENCE E. DENNIS (Vice-President for Academic Affairs, Pennsylvania State University; Chairman, Committee on Equality of Opportunity in Higher Education): Dr. Darley, I know I speak for everyone here when I say that you performed your mission this evening exceedingly well. Your address was informative and provocative, and it has set the tone for an interesting and useful discussion.

Dr. Darley has kindly consented to begin the discussion this evening by answering any questions that you might have. Please address your comments directly to him:

DAEL WOLFLE (Executive Director, American Association for the Advancement of Science): Dr. Darley, have Dr. McConnell and his staff made any studies to ascertain the real reasons students leave college? All of us speculate about the reasons for withdrawal, but no one seems to have any first-hand information.

DR. DARLEY: Dr. McConnell and his staff have not specifically studied the reasons for withdrawal, but they are beginning to look into the matter of institutional climates and their effects on individual adjustment. Dr. Stalnaker, you haven't yet analyzed the reasons for leaving, have you?

JOHN M. STALNAKER (President, National Merit Scholarship Corporation): We haven't done this yet. The numbers are still too small to yield reliable results.

DR. DARLEY: The studies of Nevitt Sanford at Vassar and the studies of Pace and Stern at Syracuse are beginning to reveal the personality determinants that relate to retention and withdrawal at particular institutions. The Pace and Stern studies, for example, relate the institutional climate to the student's needs as shown in some personality measures. Where the climate and the needs are not congruent, one would expect to find high withdrawal rates.

The Knapp-Greenbaum[1] study shows that students who go to colleges like Swarthmore, Oberlin, Carleton, and Reed have one characteristic in common: They are willing to delay their vocational choice until they complete the four years of liberal arts. They are high-ability individuals, and they are more willing to postpone vocational plans until they have attained a generous general education. These students are less driven by vocationalism or by family demands for vocationalism. They wait it out and don't drop out. Their needs do not conflict with the institutional climate.

J. KENNETH LITTLE (Associate Director, Committee on Institutional Cooperation, University of Wisconsin): We have just finished a study of 500 academically talented students who completed two years of college. We found that at the end of two years about 84 percent were still enrolled in college. For the 16 percent who withdrew, we sought the reasons. We asked the registrars what they knew, and we asked the youngster himself to tell us his story. These were actual withdrawals and not persons who transferred to any other institutions. The girls cited marriage as the major reason for withdrawal, and the boys indicated that disinterest or failure was their major reason for withdrawal. When we got the records on the whole 500, we found that their performance in college was rather undistinguished.

[1] Robert H. Knapp and Joseph J. Greenbaum, *The Younger American Scholar: His Collegiate Origins* (Chicago: University of Chicago Press, 1953).

DR. DARLEY: In terms of their potential?

DR. LITTLE: Yes, in terms of their potential. In fact, we had to go to the top 10 percent before we found a majority achieving what we would call a B or better average in college.

I would echo many of the things that you have said here tonight. One of the things that has been disturbing me as much as anything about the problem of developing manpower is the loss from high school graduation to college graduation, rather than the loss simply from high school graduation to college entrance. In other words, the problem of attrition at the college level seems to me to be as great in magnitude as it is from high school graduation to college entrance.

DR. DARLEY: The problem here, of course, is that we may be dealing with symptoms rather than reasons. I think this is what Dr. Wolfle meant. Disinterest and performance below ability may mask the more basic problems that are confronting us.

DR. LITTLE: Yes. We also found the same background factors among those who left college as among those who failed to enter college. For example, none of these dropouts had parents who had attended college. They tended to come from rural backgrounds. Or if they came from urban backgrounds, they came from families which had not had much educational advantage.

DR. DARLEY: This is precisely the kind of evidence found in Dr. Berdie's work which shows the socioeconomic and cultural factors contributing separately to the problem. But why have we as educators failed to make the importance of education clear to the child of a family in which the parents did not go to college? What have we been doing with these bright young people?

We must learn to deal with subcultural and ethnic determinants such as the custom that the first-born child must stay on the land. In a wealthy county in Minnesota, it is not lack of money but the cultural determinants of the old country that keep the children out of college. Although there is no way that we can clearly demonstrate that going to college is the best thing for every individual, there is a way to raise this issue to the level of conscious choice in minds of large numbers of students.

Why have we not been out on the highways and byways looking for ability instead of running down each other's institutions? Why have we not been saying what higher education should mean to the people, especially the students who come to us?

JOHN J. THEOBALD (Superintendent of Schools, Board of Education of the City of New York): Interestingly enough, I found the reverse of these conditions to be true in my days at Queens College, where very few of our students had parents who went to college and where we had the normal rate of dropouts. The biggest trouble we had, when we studied this problem, was finding the student's real reason for dropping out. The reason he gave the registrar was often quite different from the one we discovered later after studying the whole problem. I left college work to become a superintendent, and I have had a chance to see both sides of this problem. It seems to me that the college folk haven't undersold the importance of education at the higher-education level, but rather that we haven't started early enough in the schools to cultivate attitudes that stick when the going gets tough and other things compete. It is outside competition that pulls the kids out of college and gets them to abandon the course on which they had started but to which they were not fully committed.

DR. DARLEY: I agree, but I would like my colleagues in higher education to assume their responsibilities.

DR. THEOBALD: I agree with that.

DR. LITTLE: It is interesting that the reasons given to the registrar are often different from those given to another person.

DR. DARLEY: This takes us way back to the literature of 1890!

JOHN U. MONRO (Dean, Harvard College): I want to add a footnote to document the fact that talent losses during the college years are substantially as great as the losses between high school and college. Donald Bridgeman of the National Science Foundation has analyzed whole batches of statistics that have been gathered on this problem over the last eight or ten years, and he concludes that we lose as many talented students *in* college as on the way to college. There is apparently a much greater loss among women, but there are substantial losses among both men and women in the high-ability groups. This is a convincing set of figures, and it is terribly disturbing to anybody involved in college instruction. I think you do very well to stress this part of the problem because for years and years we have concentrated on the poor high school guidance director as the fall guy on this problem. The guidance counselor can do a great deal, but we must do better ourselves in the colleges, no doubt about that.

ELIZABETH PASCHAL (Associate Program Director, Education Division, The Ford Foundation): Dr. Darley, I may have misinterpreted something you said, but it seemed to me that you placed primary emphasis in education on the manpower problem. I wonder whether you really think that the best emphasis for education is the national need as distinct from the individual's need.

DR. DARLEY: If I left the impression, it is not the one I intended to leave. I think the task of higher education is always twofold. Since it deals with a wide range of human talent, it is called upon to solve some of our national manpower problems. Inescapably, society is using higher education more and more as its filtering, funneling, and training device. Every profession looks to the campus to meet its need through a special curriculum. Now, although it is inescapable that higher education serve this need, I would like to resist some of the extreme vocational pressures that are exerted upon it. I do not like to see a liberal arts college, after paying dutiful homage to its stated objective, announce that it offers pre-nursing, pre-this, that, or the other. It gets students coming and going on this. If it doesn't get them on the liberal arts motivation, it gets them on the vocational motivation. The state universities do the same thing. Individual needs are not best served in this way.

I did not mean to leave the impression we must serve only manpower needs. I would take John Gardner's position that we should help each student to achieve self-fulfillment, and I think this is where we fail when we stress vocational training too much. We are still telling parents if their children remain another year they will have this much more income. This is close to dishonesty. What we need to do is to convince society that higher education is itself a form of fulfillment.

CHAIRMAN DENNIS: Dr. Darley, isn't this problem of serving individual needs basically entwined with the problem of changing the intransigent curriculum?

D{sc}r. D{sc}arley: Yes. Who was it who said that trying to change a curriculum is like trying to move a graveyard? It isn't easy.

F{sc}ather A{sc}ndrew C. S{sc}mith, S.J. (President, Spring Hill College): Dr. Darley, don't those figures which you gave from the study in Wisconsin, reflecting as they do a better holding power in the private colleges as opposed to the public colleges, *support* the "myth" of size inasmuch as most of the private colleges in those states are not very large compared with the state colleges? Might it not be that the size of the college and the ability of the faculty to be acquainted with the students has something to do with the holding power?

D{sc}r. D{sc}arley: Unfortunately, the data in Minnesota show the reverse. The private colleges that we studied there were, in general, larger than the state colleges.

J{sc}ustin W. B{sc}rierly (Coordinator, College and Scholarship Counseling, Denver Public Schools): I wonder, Dr. Darley, if you would agree that many of the obstacles to higher education originate not in the college or the high school principally but in the elementary school?

D{sc}r. D{sc}arley: I am a little puzzled here because it is going to be a very short step to the family cradle! How do obstacles to higher education develop in the elementary school?

D{sc}r. B{sc}rierly: I think students do not have an adequate knowledge of their own potentialities and abilities at an early enough age. Also, I think that parents are not informed adequately or carefully enough about their children's potentialities; therefore, they do not make adequate financial and other plans to send their children to college.

It takes more than one year or two years to build proper attitudes toward higher education among both the children and their parents. You can't wait until the senior year in high school to say: "Here is a very bright student. Let's get him into college." If you do, you are five to ten years late. However, if you say the same thing five or ten years earlier, many of the financial and other obstacles would not become so formidable. Indeed, with good planning, some obstacles would never develop at all.

D{sc}r. D{sc}arley: I agree with this. Moreover, as a psychologist,

I would agree that talent can be and should be identified in the elementary school years. We have just not done a very good job.

DR. MONRO: My observations in this area lead me to the same concern about the elementary years. I am impressed by reports of how early a youngster's attitudes become firm. I have just had the good fortune of listening to Mr. Schreiber talk about the special program at Junior High School 43 in New York. He described the plan to begin the encouragement of talent in the third grade and the need to establish good, strong relationship with parents. The more I hear about this, the more sure I become that the solution of our problem depends on a three-cornered relationship among the student, the parents, and the school. The school and the parents together can do much to develop a better system of rewards to encourage good incentives. For many years, we have focused our attention on the high school guidance person. We need now to look carefully at the opening years of college, where I think we are doing a poor job, and at the early years of elementary school, where the student's attitudes seem to be shaped and, indeed, begin to harden.

I agree that we ought to improve the beachhead for youngsters landing in college, especially youngsters who do not have some kind of tradition or understanding of college behind them in the home. But this becomes quite difficult if we are dealing with attitudes that shape up early in grade school. We won't ever really solve the problem for large numbers who just never go to college unless we learn a lot more about the pattern of rewards and discouragement in the very early stages. The personality of the human being forms early.

Ten years ago I would have thought that anybody who suggested that I, as a college person, ought to worry about a youngster in the third grade was just talking through his hat. But I realize now that I must.

MRS. A. L. HENDRICK (Vice-President, Region VI, National Congress of Parents and Teachers): The organization which I represent provides an opportunity for doing what Dean Monro suggests. The 43,000 local PTA's across this country can be effective in bringing this message to parents in all grades. Instead of raising money to tune the pianos and buy curtains for the stage, local PTA groups can get parents to discuss seriously the question about which we are concerned. There are 11 million members in the organization, and they can help solve this problem, if they are alerted to it.

DONALD E. SUPER (Professor of Education, Department of Psychological Foundations and Services, Teachers College, Columbia University): I think it is important for us to keep in mind that it isn't just a matter of "talking up" the importance of going to college. The problem is really more fundamental than this. The problem is to help people to understand what one gets from college when he goes there.

DR. THEOBALD: Also, what he doesn't get there!

DR. SUPER: Agreed.

DR. BRIERLY: It seems to me that colleges and universities have failed to encourage adequate programs of college guidance in the schools. Furthermore, colleges themselves do not provide the proper type of training for persons who are to be engaged in such counseling. College counseling should begin in the elementary grades and continue until graduation from high school. Early identification and adequate training of students with college potential are the real keys to successful college guidance.

DANIEL SCHREIBER (Coordinator, Higher Horizons Program, Board of Education of the City of New York): If we feel the parents are important, then we must involve them, and we must do this when the child is in the early grades. In one way or another, we must get parents interested, if we expect to encourage real personal incentive among their children.

Problems and Responsibilities of Colleges in the Search for Talented Students: Report of a Colloquium

JOHN U. MONRO
Dean, Harvard College

I CAME TO HAVE AN INTEREST IN OUR TOPIC NOT AS A PSYCHOLOGIST, but as a financial aid officer, a teacher, and, more recently, a college dean. Although I am not competent to review the research in the field, I can report briefly the highlights of a three-day colloquium that was held under the auspices of the College Entrance Examination Board at Arden House on October 28–31, 1959.

I was struck there by a convergence of expert opinion that the success or failure of a talented young person begins very early in a youngster's life, in the early grades of primary school. We had evidence on this point from Kenneth Clark, a psychologist; from Daniel Schreiber, a schoolman; and from Sam Stouffer, a sociologist. They agreed that, while we can do some things to help later on in junior high school, high school, and college, we are dealing with a problem that goes very deep into the individual's past, indeed that gets set in the early grades of school.

Stouffer reported to us on studies of the relationship between college-going and parental attitudes. He demonstrated pretty clearly that, even when the family has enough money to pay for college, the chances are greatly diminished that the youngster will ever get there if the parents are apathetic about it. He also reported on studies of student records in school, starting in the primary grades and carrying through high school. He found that when youngsters in the top quarter of academic *ability* are not doing well in high school, they usually got off to poor starts in the grade school. Somehow they started with a disadvantage and never got over it. Stouffer reported on interviews with parents who were thought to be indifferent to higher education for their children. The interviewers found no real hostility to college, just deep ignorance about it. They concluded, however, that, if we keep at the effort to interpret the college idea to working-class families, we have a good chance to make a large breakthrough. All the talk about the advantages of higher education has begun to have an effect, and it may soon change this indifference to a live interest in college.

Stouffer's prediction was supported by Schreiber's report on successful work with the families of students in the experimental program at Junior High School No. 43 in New York. In the first year, the school staff tried to interview all the parents of the children who were in the project, and virtually all interviews had to be initiated by the school. In the second year, nine out of ten interviews were initiated by the parents! Our first conclusion, then, was that it is possible and important to discover talented youngsters in the earliest days of their schooling, to encourage them to do well, and to enlist the aid of parents in establishing goals for able students.

The next most striking piece of information we learned at Arden House concerned the heavy loss of talented students after entrance to college. This loss was documented again and again, and it was one of Dr. Darley's main points last night. He was right to stress it. Since he did, I shall not.

Another point that emerged from our discussions at Arden House concerned the degree to which we should rely on objective tests in talent hunting. Although objective tests are efficient predictive instruments, they must be used with care. The scholastic aptitude or IQ tests can mark out for us a segment of the population which has speed and accuracy in the use of certain symbols that are important for survival in college. If we pick out people from this marked-out segment of the human pie, our selections will be pretty efficient. Most of the people in this segment will succeed. Since these tests are efficient, we have learned to rely on them, and, as the numbers increase and the pressures on us increase, we shall no doubt depend on them more. The trouble is, however, that outside of this magic segment identified by the objective tests, there are many, many youngsters who can also do well in college. Many of them come from poor homes and poor schools. Our problem is that we don't know how to identify them; we don't have the right tests.

The only way to identify them now is to depend on "special advocacy," a phrase Richard King, associate director of admissions and financial aids here at Harvard, used in his report at Arden House. The special advocate may be a teacher, a principal, a minister, or one of your own staff. Sometimes an alumnus reports that although a youngster scores low, he is exceedingly able. "Special advocacy" is not a very reliable device, to say the least, but it is important for us to recognize that it is a principal channel by which a youngster with low scores gets admitted to a college.

Two other special channels bring us people to remind us regularly that there are students outside the charmed segment of high testers who can do well in college. There is the channel for competent athletes and the channel for alumni sons. Though some of these students may not test very high, they often surprise us by doing exceedingly well in college. In a period of growing reliance on tests and statistical data, it is important for us to be reminded that there are strong and good people who, for one reason or another, do badly on the tests.

Football is a special kind of advocacy. Before I leave the subject, let me point out that many colleges do exceedingly well in digging out good football players, no matter how poor the background or the school. They know how to encourage them. They advise their parents how to get them into college and how to keep them there. The barriers of deprived backgrounds, poor schooling, and bad test results, as well as the difficulties of locating talented individuals, don't bother us much, do they, when athletic talent is involved?

This ought to provoke a lot of thought. It is a kind of bad joke —a matter which should give us some feeling of guilt. But it has a hopeful aspect, too, in that we already have in existence excellent machinery for recruiting talent that we might study to advantage. Most of all, though, we need to develop new ways of discovering and measuring creativity, character, purpose, steadiness, and stamina, and other qualities that bear on success in college and later.

Donald McKinnon described for us at Arden House work he is doing at the University of California in an effort to identify creative power. He is testing adults who have already demonstrated creative power in the fields of architecture, mathematics, and scientific research, to see how these really gifted people measure on various scales. I do not pretend to understand the intricacies of his work, but I am glad that this kind of research is being done.

We shall be hearing from Mr. Schreiber about the new effort to encourage talent in the New York City schools. An important part of his message is that when a school embarks on a program of cultural enrichment, the teachers, the staff, and the whole school get excited about it. This opportunity is open to any school.

It strikes me that there is cultural aridity in lots of our country-club homes and our suburban schools, as well as in slum schools. Indeed, there is evidence that part of our talent loss occurs among students who have privileged backgrounds. The plans and hopes they derive from their families are quite often shallow in relation to their own potential. No one knows quite how to solve that problem. Of course, it is not as important in size as the problem of encouraging talent among disadvantaged groups, but it surely represents another loss of talent to our society, and I am glad to know that the problem has come under expert study.

The heart of what I have to say is that discovering and encouraging talented young people is a problem that involves every level of our schools, from the elementary grades right through college. We are losing people not just in high school and between high school and college but also in the first grade of primary school and after arrival at college. After hundreds of years of running schools and colleges, we are just now learning how to identify and encourage talented students—indeed, to define what we mean by the word "talent." It is a problem that should excite the enthusiasm of teachers throughout our educational system. It deserves our best attention, thought, research, and hard work.

The School Attrition Studies at ETS

GLEN STICE
Research Associate, Educational Testing Service

I WOULD LIKE TO TELL YOU ABOUT A PROGRAM OF RESEARCH DIRECTED toward the general problem of student attrition, or, from another point of view, motivation for education. We began this work at Educational Testing Service in 1954–55, at the request of the College Entrance Examination Board and with the support of the National Science Foundation. More recently, it has been continued with the aid of a grant from the Carnegie Corporation of New York.

The initial study concerned the plans for college of high school seniors. A second study followed up the students in the original study to find out which and how many of them actually entered college. At the present time, we are just completing a follow-up of the tenth-graders surveyed in 1955, to determine which and how many of these students have since graduated from high school. These studies have been restricted to public high school students. They have been done on students in a representative national sample stratified on the basis of school size, and the checks we have made indicate the findings are accurate.

In February and March of 1955, a short academic aptitude test and a questionnaire on family, educational and social background, and on college plans were given to 35,000 twelfth-grade and 9,700 tenth-grade students.

Based on the academic aptitude test score, students were classified in a *Very High* ability group (the most able 10 percent), a *High* ability group (the most able 30 percent), a middle ability group, and a low ability group. For those of you familiar with College Board scores, this Very High group could be expected to score 500 or higher on the Scholastic Aptitude Test. The High ability group would probably score 425 or higher.

Looking at the seniors, we found that 78 percent of boys and 62

37

percent of girls in the High ability group hoped to go to college. Thus, for the most able 325,000 seniors in 1955, approximately 230,000 expected to go to college—if not the following fall, at least eventually. Among the approximately 100,000 that did not expect to go to college, 35,000 to 40,00 were boys. In terms of aptitude, most of these 100,000 cases were among the less able of this highest one-third of the class—that is, nearer the 70th than the 90th or 100th percentile.

Plans were related to background factors. These included father's occupation, the student's vocational aspiration, family size, proportion of the student's friends who plan to go to college, his high school curriculum, class standing, and so forth. Expected relations were found. Vocational aspiration, father's occupation, and the reported proportion of friends planning college were particularly good predictors.

One year after the initial survey was completed, Dr. John W. French of Educational Testing Service, and Dr. M. C. Johnson, now at the University of Maryland, followed up on one-fifth of all seniors in the original sample to determine which of them had actually entered college. They found that 75 percent of boys and 60 percent of girls among the Very High ability group, roughly the most able 125,000 seniors, had entered one of the four-year colleges listed by the U.S. Office of Education. For the High ability group, 60 percent of boys and 46 percent of girls had entered college. You will recall, we found the previous year that 78 percent of boys and 62 percent of girls in this group *hoped* to enter college eventually. This would indicate that among the most able 325,000 seniors, about 65,000 boys and 85,000 girls did not enter college. Among the Very High ability group, the French and Johnson estimates would indicate that 16,000 boys and 25,000 girls did not enter college at once.

In evaluating these figures, several things need to be taken into consideration. First of all, it is apparent that even when we consider the narrow aptitude range represented by these two groups, there is still a high correlation with college entrance—that is, for example, the number of cases scoring between the 90th and 95th percentiles who do not go to college is appreciably less than the number scoring between the 80th and 85th percentiles who do not go to college.

Since there are still many important social roles for which a high level of ability is needed and for which college is not necessarily the most appropriate preparation, it is hardly safe to assume that all of these students stopped their formal education too soon.

Some of them may have failed to enter college not because they lacked a motivation to do so but because they had a motivation to begin training—formal or informal—for a career in politics, in labor leadership, in the performing arts, or in motherhood. All of these are surely important social roles, and it is surely in the national interest to ensure that an adequate pool of intellectually able young people are interested in and prepare for such careers. For many of these careers, the time spent at college may offer little opportunity for learning the specific vocational skills needed—for example, negotiation and winning the confidence of large publics. Thus, it may not always be wise to assume that all of these high ability non-college-goers represent a skilled manpower loss to society, or that they do not go to college because of lack of money or defective motivation.

Be that as it may, however, it should be borne in mind that these estimates of non-college-goers are probably maximum; they include all boys who joined the Armed Forces or who went to work for a year. There is some reason to believe that there is a fairly large number of such cases. Also, there is some indication that at this ability level the proportion of students entering college is higher for church-supported and independent schools.

One recent study, based on extrapolations from census data, seems to indicate that 94 percent of boys and 61 percent of girls in the Very High aptitude group enter college within the first few years after graduation, and for the High ability group these estimates are 89 percent and 58 percent respectively. Using these percentages as maximum estimates of the number of boys entering college, we might then say that of the most able 65,000 high school senior boys between 4,000 and 16,000 do not go to college. Both studies agree that of the comparable group of girls, about 25,000 do not go to college.

The next study that we did involved classifying the seniors as to whether they had entered college or not, and then looking at their background characteristics. In particular I looked at three groups: the highest 10 percent on both academic aptitude and graduation class standing; the highest 10 percent on aptitude but below the 70th percentile in graduating class standing; and those below the 50th percentile on both aptitude and achievement (that is, class standing). For the first two groups the purpose was to look for background variables that could be used as "signs"—for example, by a counselor—that a student, who presumably should, might not enter college. About 15 percent of the third low-ability, low-achievement group had entered college, and in looking at them I thought we might find some indications of presumably strong motivation.

The first thing we observed was the large number of Very High ability boys whose high school record put them below the 70th percentile in their graduating class standing. Of the 243 boys who scored in the highest 10 percent on national norms, only 69 (29 percent) were in the highest decile in their class standing; 98 (40 percent) graduated below the 70th percentile. Of the 69 boys who could be called "highest 10 percent" on both aptitude and achievement, 90 percent had entered college, but of the 98 "under-achievers," scoring equally well on the test, only 63 percent had done so. This finding probably results from several factors. We know that the academic quality of students, as well as the quality and difficulty of the curriculum, varies greatly from school to school, and I wonder if it doesn't suggest either that many very able students—faced with even more able, or more compulsively motivated, competitors—underestimate their own capacities, or that admissions officers by placing too much emphasis on rank in class are rejecting some very promising material.

When we came to look at the background correlates as predictors of college plans, the best was, of course, the question "Do you want to go to college?" Other predictors were only slightly less obvious—having a father who graduated from high school, being registered in an academic curriculum, reporting many friends to have college plans, and, of course, desiring to enter an occupation requiring college training. For the low-ability, low-achievement group, having a father in an occupation requiring a college degree was a particularly good predictor.

In detail, most of these correlates are obvious and it would have been surprising only if they had failed to appear. In total, however, they seem to suggest that the high-ability student who does not enter college is likely to be the student whose world of experience has not given him a very intimate idea of what college is all about. He sees, perhaps, a college education as of utility only in that it will increase his income. He apparently does not know "college people" well or intimately and, quite apart from the intellectual satisfactions which he may get in the laboratory or lecture hall, the idea, or perception, of living in the college social community, pursuing its interests, and interacting with its members may just simply not offer much attraction. This, of course, is speculation beyond the data. Nothing in the data that I can see contradicts it though, and a number of findings are supportive.

In the studies I have mentioned so far, the concern has been with the premature loss of talent between high school and college, but we know that losses occur at all levels. For example, of each 1,000 students who were fifth-graders in 1948–49, 893 entered the ninth grade four years later; 820 entered the tenth grade the next year; 635 entered the twelfth grade in 1955–56; and 610 graduated with the class of 1956. Since children who advanced at less or more than the normal rate, as well as those transferring to private schools, are apparently "lost" in this computation, the real loss is probably somewhat less than the indicated 39 percent. Even so, it must be appreciable, and apparently there is very little information on the relation of ability level to these figures.

Fortunately, it has recently been possible for us to trace the 9,700 sophomores whom we surveyed in 1955. We succeeded in determining whether or not approximately 9,500 of these students have since graduated. We found 7,450 had graduated and 1,960 had discontinued school before graduation.

If we look at the findings for the same ability groups used in the earlier studies, it appears that 5 percent of the Very High ability, 9 percent of the High ability, 22 percent of the middle ability, and 32 percent of the low ability sophomore boys did not graduate. For girls the comparable figures are 5, 9, 19, and 30 percent respectively. Since there were approximately 1,700,000 public high school sophomores in 1955, this would indicate that each year perhaps 5,000 to 10,000 boys and a similar number of girls, potentially able to graduate from our best colleges, do not even graduate from high school. From what information I have been able to gather, other estimates seem to indicate that this may be a conservative estimate.

The detailed tabulations for this study have just been completed, and have not yet been inspected systematically. However, it appears that in many respects the same environmental factors that are associated with the failure of high-ability graduates to enter college are also associated with pregraduation dropout. Interestingly, the ratio of graduates to dropouts is about the same for the North East, North Central, and Western census regions. For the Southern region, our data show almost twice as high a dropout rate among High ability boys as for the nation as a whole. In contrast, for the Low ability group in the South the dropout rate appears to be slightly below the national average. Looking at school- and community-size factors, apparently the very small schools and small communities retain their high-ability students at least as well as do schools as a whole. High-ability dropout seems to be concentrated in large schools and large communities. This may reflect the broader social class spectrum and the tendency of relatively disadvantaged groups to locate in the larger cities.

It is perhaps discouraging to find that 63 of the 443—about 15 percent—Very High ability boys we studied were registered in vocational and commercial curricula. (About 30 percent of the comparable group of girls were registered in vocational and commercial curricula.) Looking at students cross-classified according to aptitude and father's occupation, there are apparently few cases of the High ability sophomores who have professional parents and who fail to graduate; in our sample there were 8 out of 261. Perhaps the most surprising thing in this parent-occupation tabulation is that among the 75 Very High ability boys whose fathers were classified as "owners or administrators," 5 did not graduate. While this is only slightly above the average for the whole sample, one might have expected it to be lower. This may be an artifact of our particular sample, however.

Considering the students' vocational aspiration data, none of the Very High ability boys who wished to go into law, the humanities, medicine, or education failed to graduate; but 5 of the 100 who wanted to become engineers failed to graduate. Of the 8 Very High ability boys whose "ideal" vocational occupation was classified as "labor," 5 did not graduate. The nongraduates appear to have been slightly older than those who completed high school.

Finally, another word of caution seems in order in interpreting the percentages and estimates I have given. In the sophomore study, for example, the estimate of 5,000 to 10,000 Very High ability boys who drop out was based on only 23 cases. Because of the sample size, quite small and quite probable accidental characteristics of our sample would have resulted in rather gross changes in the resulting estimates. Furthermore, the studies were all based on a sample of schools rather than on a sample of students. Thus, the chance selection of an atypical large school would have quite substantial biasing effects.

Nevertheless, we know how our sample is biased with regard to academic aptitude, and have corrected for this in the estimates where aptitude is considered. Considering the sample as a whole we find that when our estimates are compared with census figures the results are quite close. In general, then, our impression is that our gross estimates are reasonably accurate. Some of the more specific estimates based on geographic region, parent classification, and the like are almost certainly biased to an unknown extent.

Career Attitudes: Their Nature and Correlates in Ninth Grade

DONALD E. SUPER
Professor of Education, Teachers College, Columbia University

THE CONCEPT OF CAREER DEVELOPMENT, OF VOCATIONAL DEVELOP-ment, is still a new one. Ten years ago the terms were non-existent. Today, they are frequently encountered in the professional journals of counseling psychology and of vocational guidance: a number of articles (1, 4, 7)[1] and monographs (3, 9, 10, 11) have appeared on the subject; one text (8) has used the term in its subtitle; and two major research projects, one at Columbia and one at Harvard, use the terms in their project titles. If we are to understand, as this conference seeks to, how career attitudes are formed, it is from this type of research that understanding may come. What do we mean by career attitudes?

A Study of Vocational Maturity

In 1951 I began a study (6, 7) which provides something of an answer to these questions at the point of the first prevocational decisions, grade nine. Schools are so organized that, in the ninth grade, boys and girls are required to make choices between continuing their education and leaving school, between education for higher or for the lower-level occupations, between education for technical or for nontechnical fields, between general and vocational education. We defined the basic career attitude as vocational maturity, as readiness, that is, to cope with the vocational developmental tasks of one's life stage and as the appropriateness of the behavior manifested in dealing with these tasks. The questions in this study were: how mature vocationally, how ready to make the required choices of educational and vocational-preparatory programs, are boys reaching the first critical choice-point in their lives, and to what is this maturity related?

[1] See Bibliography, p. 51.

The Career Pattern Study used as its subjects all of the boys who, in 1951–52, were in the ninth grade of the public schools of Middletown, New York. About 70 miles northwest of New York City, Middletown has a population of about 23,000; it is, economically and sociologically, an average town. There were 142 boys; data for 105 typical boys were used for the present analysis. Their average age was fourteen. They came from all social classes. Our data included tests and questionnaires, the administration of which required about two school days, four hours of interviews which had been tape-recorded and transcribed, and teachers' grades and reports.

A preliminary list of nineteen possible indices or measures of vocational maturity (that is, of the maturity of behavior in dealing with the problems of prevocational and vocational choice) at age fourteen was drawn up. Some of these have often been used: for example, agreement of a person's actual IQ with the intellectual level typical of persons in the occupation to which he aspires is a common index of realism or maturity of vocational choice. We developed several such measures of realism.

For some of the other possible manifestations of vocational maturity, no available or readily adapted measures existed, and considerable time was devoted to devising methods of analyzing the content of our interviews in order to obtain indices of these variables. In the end, we had our nineteen measures for each boy. They were grouped, after some preliminary work, in five major categories, as follows:

> Orientation to Vocational Choice
> Consistency of Vocational Preferences
> Crystallization of Traits
> Independence of Work Experience
> Wisdom of Vocational Preferences

The next step was to ascertain whether or not our nineteen presumed indices of vocational maturity, grouped in these five categories, agreed with each other. If the theorizing was good, the correlations among the indices in a given category would be moderately high, and there would also be some relationship between the indices in one category and those in any other: these last might be low, but if all our measures were indeed indices of vocational maturity they would, as measures of the same basic characteristic, show some agreement.

The four measures of Orientation to Vocational Choice were, in fact, significantly related to each other. Our reasoning so far appeared sound: concern with prevocational and vocational choices, acceptance of responsibility of choice and planning, having information about the preferred occupation, and having done some planning for preparation or entry into that occupation, may be manifestations of vocational maturity in ninth-grade boys. So also may a fifth index added later, assessing the Use of Resources in Vocational Orientation.

But none of our other presumed indices of vocational maturity stood the test of congruent or construct validity, for the correlations between the other fourteen measures, and between these fourteen and the five measures which did stand the test, were about zero. The three measures of Consistency of Vocational Preferences, the five measures of Crystallization of Vocationally Relevant Traits, the one measure of Independence of Work Experience, and the five measures of Wisdom of Vocational Preferences, agreed neither with other measures in the same category nor with indices in other categories.

This does not mean that consistency of vocational preferences, or agreement between actual and required intelligence, or the other measures, may not be good predictors of later adjustment or valid indices of vocational maturity at other age levels: our data do not, as yet, tell us. But the Career Pattern Study findings in grade nine, at age fourteen, do strongly suggest that at this age, when youth is called upon to make decisions which affect not only the level but the field of effort and attainment, vocational maturity does not consist of having a stable occupational preference, of having clear-cut vocational interests, of having had significant work experience, of having abilities or interests or economic resources which are appropriate to one's aspirations.

Vocational development appears to have reached a point at which one can expect a boy to show some orientation to the problem or necessity of ultimate occupational choice. Boys who manifest some concern with the choice problem tend to accept responsibility for playing a part in the making of vocational choices and plans; they tend also to have information about the occupation which interests them most and to have done some planning concerning that occupation. The concern is often shallow, the responsibility may have been little exercised, the information possessed is limited, and so is the planning. But these are the operative career attitudes at this life stage. Vocational choice, or even prevocational choices, at this stage, are likely to be premature.

Since this may seem to be a somewhat dogmatic statement, let me cite two further analyses by way of justification. One concerns a factor analysis of our presumably good measures of vocational maturity, the other an attempt at developing normative material for this age.

The four vocational maturity indices which were shown to have substantial construct validity, and the index of independence of work experience, consist of a total of 27 subscores. These were submitted to factor analysis. Five factors were extracted, one of which corresponded with the index of independence of work experience, while the others appeared largely in the subscores which constituted the four measures of vocational maturity. But the factors suggest a somewhat different psychological structure, for one of them appears to be a somewhat general vocational maturity factor which might best be named "planfulness"; the second, "taking the long view ahead"; the third, the "short view"; and the fourth, the "intermediate view." This analysis, like our first, suggests that vocational maturity at age fourteen consists of a planning approach to life adjustment problems.

At age fourteen, concern with the need to make choices is fairly widespread, but the tendency is to focus on the more immediate choices. The concern tends thus to be more with choice of school courses for the next semester or the next year than with the total pattern and sequence of the exploratory and preparatory years, or with the kind of education to pursue after completing the present school program, or with the kind of occupation to enter after college, or with the kind of position one might hold after an apprenticeship.

The analysis of the information possessed by these fourteen-year-olds about the occupation of their preference revealed considerable information about occupational requirements, but very limited information concerning duties and conditions of work and other post-entry matters. This suggests that many boys may be aspiring to occupations which they would, after entry, find distasteful. The level of planning was also rather low, for more than one-half had apparently done little about getting information on which to base high school plans, about one-third had made no plans which related high school study to preferred occupation, and post-high-school planning was about equally lacking.

At the same time, acceptance of responsibility for choice and planning was rather widespread, most of these boys believing that they had a major role to play in choosing and planning their occupations. Their concern with immediate choices and their limited information and planning suggest that they were about ready to exercise a responsibility which they had not thus far really assumed.

Although realism of vocational choice was found to be unrelated to any other presumed measure of vocational maturity at this age, it should be worthwhile to examine the data for realism of preferences, when this realism is judged by the aptitudes and interests which are typical of people in a given type of work. Almost one-half of these fourteen-year-old boys had aptitudes which were appropriate to their aspirations, but rather more than one-half of the group would like to enter occupations in which they are very likely to experience difficulties arising from lack of aptitude. Almost half of the boys had vocational aspirations which did not agree with their interests as measured by a vocational interest inventory. That the realism measures agreed with nothing else suggests that a substantial number of the agreements which do exist between personal characteristics and occupational requirements may be fortuitous. If this is indeed so, then vocational development has not, in this culture and at this age, reached a point at which boys are ready to make choices of the level or field of occupation, or, therefore, of level or field of education which is more or less directly occupationally oriented.

Our second question is, how are these career attitudes developed? To phrase the question more modestly, what are the correlates of maturity in these ninth-graders?

Variables Associated with Vocational Maturity

One way of getting an understanding of how to improve vocational orientation is to ascertain the variables which are associated with vocational maturity. Some of the factors which are correlated with vocational maturity may be related to it in a causative manner: if so, then providing boys and girls with needed experiences may improve their career attitudes.

In the Career Pattern Study twenty-eight such variables were examined, including intelligence, socioeconomic status, family relationships, and achievement in school work and in extracurricular activities. The results make it possible to describe the vocationally mature ninth-grade boy as one who tends to have the following characteristics:

He lives in an *intellectually stimulating environment,* as shown by placement on the upper-middle or middle socioeconomic levels, by a variety of activities in and out of the home which are rich in cultural content, by the taking of the more intellectually demanding courses in school, and by coming from an urban rather than from a rural environment;

He has the *mental ability* which is helpful, if not essential, in responding to the stimulation of this environment;

He responds to the stimuli which surround him by *aspiring* to a high- rather than to a low-level occupation;

He *expects to make good* his aspirations, looking forward with some confidence to entering his preferred field of work and to making good in it;

He *habitually achieves* by getting good grades, taking part in school clubs and activities and getting elected to positions of leadership, belonging to outside organizations, and doing things which require or demonstrate and develop a degree of independence from the home and family.

As all of these relationships, while significant, are somewhat low (none of the correlations are higher than .40), there are obviously vocationally mature boys who do not have some of these characteristics.

Knowing some of the variables which tend to be associated with vocational maturity at age fourteen, what are the implications for career attitude development?

Implications for Vocational Development

A *stimulating environment* can be provided by a variety of institutions. Although the home is a major factor, and overcoming the effects of a culturally impoverished home is often difficult for other agencies, a major function of the school is to provide the intellectual and cultural resources which many homes lack. A school may well ask itself not only with what knowledge and skills it should equip its pupils, but also with what experiences it, with resources generally greater than those of the home, should provide its pupils in order to foster their development. If the family does not have a variety of magazines and books, space and equipment for arts and crafts, opportunities to appreciate music and art, contact with the world of science, an awareness of civic responsibility and of current events, and so forth, the school does or should. These resources can be used to stimulate career development.

Intellectual resources can be stimulated or allowed to stagnate and atrophy: if a stimulating environment is provided the chances of intellectual development are maximized.

The *aspiring* attitudes of the vocationally mature youth suggest the value of an encouraging, positive approach on the part of the school. If growth is not possible in one direction, another outlet must be found or stultification will result. Hence one function of the school is to help the pupil find goals to which he can legitimately aspire, and to which he will aspire because of their real attraction.

The *expectation of success* is closely related to aspiring to appropriate goals. If the child's education is so planned and directed that it consists of establishing and working toward such goals with suitable direction and resources, he should experience success. With the habit of success comes the expectation of success which tends to characterize the vocationally mature ninth-grader.

These seem, then, to be the principles which may be derived from the Career Pattern Study data. I am sure that they do not constitute a complete and sufficient set of principles for the fostering of career attitudes in early adolescents. It is quite possible that our list of variables studied omitted some which are quite important in vocational development, and that our list of principles, derived from incomplete data, is therefore incomplete. And yet I must confess that I prefer an incomplete set of principles based on facts to a theoretically more complete set of principles further removed from reality.

BIBLIOGRAPHY

1. BEILIN, H. "The Application of General Developmental Principles to the Vocational Area," *Journal of Counseling Psychology,* II (1953), 53–57.
2. BÜHLER, CHARLOTTE. *Der menschlishes Lebenslauf als psychologisches Problem.* Leipzig: Hirzel, 1933.
3. GINZBERG, E., *et al. Occupational Choice.* New York: Columbia University Press, 1953.
4. HOLLAND, J. L. "A Theory of Vocational Choice," *Journal of Counseling Psychology,* VI (1959), 35–44.
5. LEHMAN, H. C. *Age and Achievement.* Princeton, N.J.: Princeton University Press, 1953.
6. MERTON, R. K., *et al. The Student Physician.* Cambridge, Mass.: Harvard University Press, 1957.
7. SUPER, D. E. *The Psychology of Careers.* New York: Harper & Bros., 1957.
8. ———. "A Theory of Vocational Development," *American Psychologist,* VIII (1953), 185–90.
9. SUPER, D. E., and BACHRACH, P. B. *Scientific Careers and Vocational Development Theory.* New York: Bureau of Publications, Teachers College, Columbia University, 1957.
10. SUPER, D. E., and OVERSTREET, PHOEBE L. *The Vocational Maturity of Ninth-Grade Boys.* New York: Bureau of Publications, Teachers College, Columbia University, 1960.
11. SUPER, D. E., *et al. Vocational Development: A Framework for Research.* New York: Bureau of Publications, Teachers College, Columbia University, 1957.

The Kansas Surveys of Postgraduation Activities of High School Seniors

ALEX A. DAUGHTRY

Chairman, Division of Teacher Education,
Kansas State Teachers College at Emporia

THE KANSAS SURVEYS OF POSTGRADUATION ACTIVITIES OF HIGH school seniors resulted from a rather casual question asked during a staff meeting at Kansas State Teachers College, Emporia. This question was: What percent of the Kansas high school graduates go immediately to college?

We thought that the information was surely available somewhere in the state, but we found that this was not the case. Furthermore, a review of research in the area of college-going on the part of high school graduates convinced us that the specific information we sought was not readily available on a nation-wide basis.

We concluded that this would be a fruitful field for exploration, so a comprehensive survey of the graduates of 1955 was planned. The basic purpose was to determine the activities entered into by members of the graduating group, but we decided also to gather information concerning those students who seemed to be superior in ability.

Similar studies have been made of the 1956, 1957, and 1958 classes, although the latter two have not included an investigation of the superior students. Detailed reports of the first three studies have been printed; the 1958 report will be published soon, and the 1959 study is under way.

Data for the studies were obtained directly from high school principals in 1955 and 1956, and through the State Department of Public Instruction in 1957 and 1958. Incidentally, we have had excellent cooperation from both public school officials and state department administrators in carrying on these surveys. We think that one desirable outcome of the studies has been an increased interest on the part of secondary school administrators and guidance workers in gathering information concerning their graduates.

We found in 1955 that 40 percent of the Kansas high school graduates enrolled in a college or university in the fall following completion of high school. This percentage dropped slightly, to 39, in 1956. It rose to 41 percent for the 1957 graduates, however, and to 43 percent in 1958.

Time does not permit a detailed analysis of the findings of the state-wide studies. There are several aspects of our findings, however, which I think will be of interest to you in connection with the theme of this conference. It should be borne in mind that these conclusions have to do with *all* graduating seniors, not just those who seemed to be superior in ability.

First, we found a considerable difference between the college-going record of boys and that of girls. The difference in percentage points has ranged consistently from 10 to 12, with male graduates continuing their education in greater numbers. This is in accord with the results of most studies of this type.

Second, we found that there was tremendous variation among the high schools of the state with respect to the percent of graduates who went to college. Individual school percentages ranged from zero to 100. In part, this results from the fact that Kansas has many small high schools—more than half of all of the high schools in the state are under 75 in total enrollment. But this is not the complete explanation for the variation. Because we have continued these studies over a period of years, we have been able to observe that certain high schools, both large and small, have a consistent record of sending or not sending their graduates to college. The challenging aspect of this situation is that there seems to be "no rhyme nor reason" to the differences which exist. Two communities, located only a few miles from each other, similar in socioeconomic background and in outward appearances, may be at opposite extremes in the matter of encouraging their high school graduates to continue formal education.

This same variation exists on a county-wide basis, as well as on an individual school basis. Kansas has 105 counties, with one to twenty high schools in each. The county percentages ranged from 4 percent to 61 percent in 1957, and similar variations were found in the earliest studies. Surprisingly, the location of the county seems to have little influence on the record which it establishes in sending its high school graduates to college. Aside from the fact that counties which have higher education institutions compile above-average records in this respect, there is no pattern of relationship between geographic location and the rate of college attendance.

A third point which has become apparent is that graduates of larger high schools tend to go to college in greater numbers than do graduates of small high schools. Again, it should be kept in mind that Kansas is a state of small secondary schools. When we speak of "large" high schools, we are thinking of those which enroll more than 475 pupils. Schools in this group send about half of their graduates to college, while the "small" schools—under 150 in enrollment—send fewer than one-third.

A fourth finding has to do with the relationship between the location of the high school and the percent of its graduates enrolling in college. According to our surveys, the "proximity factor" is important in Kansas only if the high school is located within ten miles of a college or university. We found little or no difference among high schools located ten to twenty-five miles, twenty-five to fifty miles, fifty to one hundred miles, and more than one hundred miles, from the nearest institution of higher education. Our conclusion has been that beyond an easy commuting range of ten miles, distance from a college campus is not an important factor in whether or not a Kansas boy or girl goes to college. This may be due in part to the fact that Kansas has only one four-year college in the western half of the state, so Kansans have been accustomed to sending their sons and daughters some distance from home to obtain a college education.

Thus far, my remarks have pertained to all graduates of Kansas high schools. I thought it appropriate to include them, even though we are primarily concerned at this conference with "talented but disadvantaged youth," because the findings in general would apply to some extent to this particular group. Now I would like to turn our attention to the phase of the studies which had to do with students who seemed to be superior in ability. As was previously stated, this phase of the study was made in its most complete form in 1955, repeated to some extent in 1956, but not included in the 1957 or 1958 surveys.

Our first problem was to identify the superior students. We met this problem by studying three groups: first, the graduates who were valedictorians and salutatorians of their graduating classes; second, the graduates who ranked in the upper third of their classes; and third, the graduates who ranked at or above the 67th percentile on the Kansas High School Senior Comprehensive Examination.

The first group included 930 individuals, with smaller schools represented to a greater extent than larger ones. Principals were asked to report whether or not these individuals had enrolled in college, and it was found that 62 percent of them had done so. This percentage may be compared with the over-all percentage of 40 for the entire graduating group of 1955. Principals were also asked to report the reasons for valedictorians and salutatorians not attending college. In almost a third of the cases, "matrimony" was the reason given. Second in importance was the "lack of financial backing," accounting for 18 percent. "No desire to continue education" accounted for 13 percent of those who did not go on. There could be questions raised, of course, concerning the accuracy of the information furnished by the high school principals, but we must conclude that their opinions have some validity.

With respect to graduates who ranked in the upper third of their classes, it was found that approximately two-thirds continued their education. Again, there were differences according to size of school, with the smallest schools reporting an average of 60 percent and the largest reporting 75 percent. No attempt was made to get information concerning this group beyond the fact that the individual student did or did not go to college.

The use of rank in class as a method of identifying graduates who seemed to be superior in ability is subject to question, as far as Kansas is concerned, because of the large number of small high schools. A school which graduates only three individuals has one in the upper third, one in the middle third, and one in the lower third, but all may be about equal in ability as far as academic achievement is concerned—and in comparison with other schools, all three may be superior or inferior. This portion of the study was included, however, on the assumption that in spite of its limitations it would contribute to the over-all findings.

The third group included students who ranked at or above the 67th percentile on the Kansas High School Senior Comprehensive Examination. This is a test provided by the Bureau of Measurements of Kansas State Teachers College to any high school which wishes to make use of it. It consists of a general ability test and a battery of four achievement tests in the fields of English, science, social science, and mathematics. This is a voluntary program, but in 1955 about 14,000 (or 70 percent) of the high school seniors in Kansas took it.

Our method of selecting superior students yielded a group of 3,386 individuals, or about one-fourth of the total number of seniors taking the test. It was found that 65 percent of these graduates had gone to college. Again, there were variations according to size of school, with the smaller schools lagging behind the larger ones. Three-fourths of the boys in the superior group continued their education, while only slightly more than half of the girls did so.

As a part of this phase of the study, principals were asked to identify the occupation of the student's father or mother. The replies were grouped in five categories used first by Dael Wolfle —professional and semiprofessional; managerial; sales, clerical, and service; farmer; factory, craftsmen, unskilled, and similar occupations.[1] Our findings confirmed those of Dr. Wolfle, in that the children of parents in the professional and semiprofessional group went to college in larger numbers than did children of parents in other groups.

We made an attempt to get information directly from the

[1] Dael Wolfle, *America's Resources of Specialized Talent* (New York: Harper & Bros., 1954), p. 160.

superior students who did not continue their education. High school principals could give us mailing addresses on 814 such graduates, and 364 of them returned inquiry forms to us. A detailed report of their responses is included in the printed study; briefly, we found that financial reasons were chiefly responsible for the fact that these students did not go to college. A considerable number of them indicated that they planned to continue their education at a later date.

In general, our investigation with respect to graduates who seemed to be superior in ability led to the conclusion that about two-thirds of the upper one-third of Kansas high school graduates do go immediately to college. While this may seem to be encouraging, it must be remembered that the one-third which does not go on includes approximately 2,500 young people who have demonstrated above-average academic ability. Neither Kansas nor the nation can afford to ignore the potential of this group. This, I gather, is our reason for being here today.

Wisconsin Study of Academically Talented High School Graduates: Their College Plans and Progress

J. KENNETH LITTLE

Associate Director, Committee on Institutional Cooperation, University of Wisconsin

THIS IS A REPORT OF THE HIGHLIGHTS OF A TWO-YEAR STUDY OF academically talented youth who graduated from Wisconsin high schools in the spring of 1957. The study included: (1) a survey in spring 1957 of their plans for education beyond high school; (2) a follow-up survey of their parents in the fall of 1957 to learn what these graduates were actually then doing and what the parents thought about the value of college education; (3) a follow-up survey in the winter of 1958 of those who were not attending college to learn what their occupations were, and whether they then had college plans; and (4) a follow-up survey in the spring of 1959 of those who had entered colleges in fall 1957 to learn about their progress and persistence in college studies.

An academically talented graduate was defined as one who had ranked in the top fourth of his class both on a test of mental aptitude and in rank in high school studies. Under this definition, about 15 percent of the high school graduates qualified. In this group there were three girls for each two boys.

Some of the major findings of these studies were:

1. The number of academically talented youth who enrolled in college in the fall term immediately following their graduation was 93 percent of the number who reported plans to attend college.

2. The number of the academically talented who did not enroll, or were not likely to enroll in a degree-granting college was between 15 percent and 20 percent of the boys and between 35 percent and 40 percent of the girls. About 15 percent of the girls, and 2 percent of the boys entered training programs of a nondegree type.

3. Heavy majorities of the academically talented graduates were going to college regardless of size of high school, level of reported family income, occupation of father, level of educational attainment of parents, or distance from a college opportunity.

4. An overwhelming majority (95 percent) of the parents of the academically talented voted that a college education is worth making the financial sacrifice it requires and that too many young people who deserve to go to college are not able to do so. Very few believed that too many young people are going to college or that college is not worthwhile for many who go.

Many of their sons or daughters, however, reported that their parents were indifferent about their going to college. Of those not going to college only 58 percent reported that their parents wanted them to go; the other 42 percent reporting that their parents did not care. This difference in strength of parental encouragement consistently distinguished the college-going from the non-college-going groups of graduates. Parents of graduates who were not attending college cited two major reasons: (1)

could not afford it, 33 percent; (2) graduate did not want to go, 25 percent.

5. The academically talented boys who did not go to college were typically found to be in clerical, unskilled or semiskilled, or service occupations. The majority of them were not satisfied with their job prospects. Three-fourths of them were planning or hoping to get further education or training. Some were enrolled in correspondence courses, others in evening programs of colleges or vocational schools. They stressed the economic necessity of further education for job advancement and sought the greater understanding and enjoyment which they thought that more schooling would bring. The academically talented girls were usually found to be in office and clerical work. In contrast to the boys, three-fourths of them were satisfied with their work and its prospects. The prospects frequently included marriage. Slightly more than one-fourth had plans for further education. Only 8 percent expected to go to college in the near future, as compared with 77 percent of the boys. A fourth of the girls reported that they were glad that they did not continue schooling.

About one-fifth of both boys and girls said that they did not continue school because they could not afford it; a tenth of the boys and three-tenths of the girls said they would not attend college even if they had the money.

6. Nearness to a college was not sufficient in itself to induce some academically talented graduates to attend college. Low levels of parental education, the influence of non-college-going peers, and attitudes of indifference toward school and school work were negative influences which outweighed the influence of living in a college community and the opportunity to attend college while living at home.

7. The following thumbnail sketches generalize the differences between the academically talented youth who attend college and those who do not.

The typical top-ranking youth who was *planning to go to college* came from a home in which the father was at least a high school graduate. The father may have been employed in any one of the major occupations. The family income was at least average among the families of the community, and the family was able to contribute more than $500 toward his college expenses. The youth had applied for a scholarship and would borrow money for college expenses, if necessary. He may have graduated from a high school of any size, but, whatever the school, he had found his high school studies interesting. His parents had strongly encouraged him to go to school, and his teachers had identified him as having unusual promise in some special field. His friends were going to college. He had taken a college preparatory course which had included studies in mathematics, science, and foreign languages. He aspired to professional or executive positions in the occupational world. He wanted to increase his knowledge and skills, and had never thought that he would not go to college.

The typical top-ranking youth who was *not planning to attend college* came from a home in which the father was a farmer or semiskilled worker who had never attended college. His family had average or below average income and could contribute less than $500 toward his college expenses. The youth believed that his parents could not afford to send him to school. He was attending a small high school. He was less interested in school studies than his college-going classmates of equal ability, and his parents were less interested in his going to college. Most of his friends were, like him, getting jobs. He did not want to borrow money for college expenses even if he could pay it back on the installment plan. In fact, there is some doubt that he would go to college even if he could afford it. He had not applied for a scholarship. He had not been identified by his teachers as a student who had shown unusual achievement or promise in a specific field. He hoped some day to be an executive or skilled worker. He believed that success depended upon ability plus hard work, and he wanted to go to work and start earning money quickly.

8. A follow-up of about 500 academically talented youth who entered college in the fall of 1957 showed that they had entered more than 100 different colleges. After two academic years, about 73 percent were still enrolled in the college of their original enrollment. About 12 percent had transferred to another school, and 15 percent had discontinued college studies. The discontinuances frequently came from homes in which the parents had

not attended college. The primary reason for discontinuance was scholastic difficulty or disinterest, with marriage playing a strong role among girls.

9. The scholastic performance of the total group of academically talented graduates was undistinguished. More than a fourth had earned scholastic averages in the lower half of their college classmates, and less than a half had averages which placed them in the top 30 percent. Academic difficulties were occurring despite apparently strong high school preparation as judged by the patterns of high school studies presented at time of admission.

10. If a "B or better" average is used as the criterion for superior college work, 75 percent of those who attained this level had ranked in the top 10 percent of their classes in both mental test score and high school rank; but a third of those who did so rank in the top 10 percent failed to attain a B or better average.

11. If the findings of this study of the college persistence of academically talented were true among all such students, the attrition of such graduates from high school graduation to college graduation would be about 25 percent among boys and 50 percent among girls.

Conclusions

1. The persistent and pervasive way in which the sociocultural background of the families, especially the educational attainment of the parents, conditions the educational aspirations and attitudes of the high school graduates is perhaps the most striking finding about factors which influence the decisions about college attendance. In every phase of this study, this influence stands in bold relief, and must be given priority over economic means as a general determinant of college attendance. This priority does not deny existence of financial barriers which deter the college attendance of highly capable youth, but the economic barriers are interwined with such factors as inadequacy of knowledge about opportunities for self-help, loans or scholarships, or lack of knowledge about, or strong interest in, what colleges offer to them.

2. In general, the cultural level and educational attainment of parents, the attitudes and values of close friends, and the psychosocial characteristics of the graduates themselves outweigh such

factors as size or strength of a high school program, nearness to a college, or family income as influences upon decisions to attend college. Counseling programs must reach parents as well as students.

3. The number of topflight boys who do not now go to college is smaller than previously believed, but the loss between high school graduation and college graduation is considerable. The failure of many girls of exceptional promise to go to school and the general attitude among parents and girls that a college education is not important for women suggests an area of special importance for research and educational programming.

4. The problems of transition from high school to college are serious. Too many able college students are dropping from schools because of academic maladjustment. In many colleges, these problems are as pressing as the financial problems, and have implications for curriculum and instruction in college as much as for patterns of high school preparation.

5. Tests of scholastic aptitude and rank in class are commonly used to identify academically talented youth. Such measures define the pool within which such youth are most frequently found. Research needs to be directed, however, toward determining whether there is a definable floor or minimum for such measures, beyond which other qualities of the individual become more determinative of high-level attainment, and what these qualities are. Remarkable differences in persistence in studies, high-level productivity, and creativity exist among students who have equally high scholastic aptitude test scores and marks in their studies. All of these students may shine, but some of them sparkle. The research should be directed at the qualities and circumstances which produce sparkle.

In the drive for the identification and better education of talented youth, these studies remind us that human aptitudes, promise, and worth have dimensions not revealed by the IQ or grade point average. Given students who possess the basic intelligence and inclinations found in most college graduates, other human qualities seem crucial in determining ultimate achievement. Current research upon the dimensions of intelligence and the qualities which underlie outstanding human achievement bear watching. Pending more definitive knowledge than now possessed about human promise, the wise course, in my opinion, is to provide abundant opportunity for outstanding human ability to rise at any stage in the educational process, and to counsel all students and their parents always to keep the door open to further educational training. An open-ended educational program is imperative for talented youth.

In terms of the unpredictable demands of a fast changing and increasingly scientific and technological world, it is wise counsel for all youth.

Factors Related to Educational Discontinuance of Arkansas High School Seniors

FRANCIS STROUP
Associate Professor of Physical Education,
Northern Illinois University

WHILE EMPLOYED AT SOUTHERN STATE COLLEGE, I, ALONG WITH Dr. D. C. Andrew, served as project director for a two-year study of factors related to educational discontinuance of Arkansas high school seniors. This study was supported by the Cooperative Research Branch of the U.S. Office of Education.

Most of the information for the study was gained from questionnaires returned by more than 12,000 representative high school seniors of the state. Other information used in the study included the scores these seniors had previously made on the American Council on Education Psychological Examination as well as data regarding subsequent college enrollment provided by administrators of the colleges in which the respondents were thought by their high school principals to be enrolled.

This unusually rigorous method of determining whether or not a respondent entered college probably contributed to the relatively small percent of students who were identified as college enrollees.

The study revealed that while about 45 percent of all respondents indicated plans to go to college, only about 26 percent were found to be enrolled in college the fall semester following their graduation from high school.

Some of the factors related to educational discontinuance may be deduced from the following comparisons: Boys went to college in greater proportion than girls; white students went in greater proportion than colored students; seniors from larger schools and from schools with the highest academic rating went in greater proportions than seniors from schools with smaller enrollments and with lower academic ratings; students living in cities and towns went to college in greater proportions than did those living in rural areas; younger seniors went in greater proportion than older seniors; and students from families in the higher income brackets went in greater proportions than those from families in the lower brackets.

More than 46 percent of the seniors who had scored above the median on the ACE test attended college while less than 21 percent of those who had scored below the median attended. And more than 56 percent of the seniors who followed a college preparatory curriculum in high school attended college compared to 22 percent attendance, or less, for students who followed other high school curricula.

A rich home environment, a family tradition of college attendance, a decision by the senior to follow a profession, participation by the senior in school organizations and on athletic teams were all found to be positively related to college attendance.

In order that trends related to ACE scores might be more closely observed, respondents were divided into three groups according to the percentile ranks of their ACE scores. These groups were designated as terciles and this grouping again verified the correlation between ACE scores and college attendance.

The upper tercile—like the group who followed the college preparatory course in high school—contained about 56 percent who later went to college. But when membership in the two groups was examined and only students who were members of *both* the upper tercile and the college preparatory group were considered, more than 70 percent were found to have enrolled in college. This sharp rise in percentage of college attendance accompanying membership in the *two* groups over membership in *either* group vividly illustrates the importance of multiple relationships between factors related to college attendance. And this multiple relationship seems of extreme importance in making predictions or in solving problems related to college attendance.

For too long we have been prone to make predictions regarding college attendance on the basis of a single known factor. But to conclude that an Arkansas high school senior has only one chance in four to attend college because that was the average for the state is as ill-founded as to say that Ted Williams, in his heyday, had but one chance in 35 times at bat to hit a home run because that was the average for the Boston team. The Arkansas study provided evidence that a reasonable basis for predicting college attendance for any individual is his membership in *several* groups for which a known relationship to college attendance is available.

The identification of factors related to college attendance and the verification of the operation of the principle of multiple relationship between these factors led to the suggestion of a ten-item College Proneness Test which the investigators thought offered promise as a simple instrument providing a tangible index for describing the probability of an individual's entering college.

A student's status regarding some of these factors related to college attendance is alterable; regarding others, it is not. An example of an unalterable factor is sex. But the financial ability of a student to attend college, the high school he attends, and the curriculum he follows in high school are alterable factors. The best approach to improving the probability of a student's entering college seems to be the early identification and the early removal of some of these alterable barriers to college attendance.

Of the barriers identified in the study, the one which can be removed most easily for a given individual by overt, external assistance is the one related to economic status. And through programs of scholarships, grants, and loans, much progress has been made in overcoming this barrier. But through the years, such programs have consistently provided aid for students *after* graduation from high school—which in most cases is after decisions regarding college attendance have already crystallized. And the fact that this conference was planned and is being held is evidence that financial aid to high school graduates has not in itself provided a satisfactory solution to the problem.

Some barriers to college attendance are so pronounced in their cultural orientation that progress in their removal—like the grinding of the mills of God—will be extremely slow. Dr. Conant's suggestion that high schools with graduating classes of less than a hundred students be eliminated will be decades in its fulfillment. Yet each year will find many talented seniors attending such schools—seniors who will not be able to surmount this barrier to college attendance. Consequently their full potential will never be developed and the nation will be the loser.

The problem of increasing the probability of college attendance by removing certain barriers for such students was recognized in the report of the Arkansas study and a recommendation worthy of the attention of this conference was made regarding its solution. This recommendation was that selected, academically talented students who were disadvantaged by living in school districts not providing schools of the highest academic classification and served by schools not offering a college preparatory curriculum be given both moral and financial encouragement to attend a nearby school that provides these opportunities.

Such a proposal is consistent with repeated findings that attitudes and decisions affecting college attendance take form long before the senior year in high school. The proposed plan also provides an approach for the salvaging of talented individuals without awaiting the distant day when institutional changes will have been effected.

A pilot program beginning now and functioning in limited geographic areas would test the validity of this recommendation and would also provide an opportunity to observe and solve the operational problems which might confront a national program of this nature should such a national program be attempted.

Why Capable Indiana High School Students Do Not Continue Their Schooling

WENDELL W. WRIGHT

Professor of Education, Indiana University

STUDENTS, PARENTS, AND HIGH SCHOOL OFFICIALS WERE INTERVIEWED in an effort to determine the reasons why certain youths who ranked in the upper 10 percent of the 1955 high school graduating classes of Indiana did not continue their education beyond the high school. Of this group of students, 875 were included in the study.

In the upper 10 percent of the Indiana high school graduating classes for 1955, the girls outnumbered the boys slightly more than two to one (2,343 girls and 1,136 boys).

Of the 1955 Indiana high school graduates ranking in the upper 10 percent, 71 percent continued their education beyond the high school, and, by the beginning of the second year following graduation, another 2 percent had started to continue their education. The boys in the upper 10 percent continued beyond the high school in 85 percent of the cases, whereas the girls continued in only 64 percent of the cases.

Of the 29 percent (1,011) who did not continue their education, 75 percent were engaged in full-time employment, 21 percent of the girls were married, 18 percent of the boys were in military service, and less than 5 percent of all students were unemployed, unknown, or deceased.

Of the fathers, 37.2 percent had completed the twelfth grade, while 32.2 percent had not gone beyond the eighth grade. Of the mothers, 44.2 percent had completed the twelfth grade, while 26.0 percent had not gone beyond the eighth grade. In only 2.2 percent of the cases had either parent completed the sixteenth year or above, and in slightly more than 8 percent of the cases had either parent completed a grade above the twelfth.

In 43.4 percent of the cases, the family's yearly income was in excess of $5,000 as reported by the high school official; in 37.3 percent of the cases it was from $3,500 to $5,000; and in 19.2 percent of the cases it was less than $3,500.

In the opinion of the school officials, 70 percent of the youths lived in school communities in which the attitude toward going to college was favorable.

Of the youths who were employed, less than 10 percent earned $75 or more weekly; slightly less than 60 percent earned $50 to $74 weekly; about 30 percent earned $35 to $49 weekly; and approximately 2 percent earned less than $35. More than nine in ten youths liked their present employment and planned to continue in the work.

Only 28.8 percent of the boys were enthusiastic about the academic phase of school as compared with 38 percent of the girls, and considerably more boys (17 percent) than girls (5.3 percent) indicated that they were only mildly interested or indifferent. In the opinion of school officials, 52.3 percent of the girls and 33.9 percent of the boys were enthusiastic about the academic part of school.

There was a college orientation program of some kind in 90 percent of the schools in which the youths were enrolled. As many as 78.1 percent of the youths had discussed further education with some school official. Ninety percent of the boys and 79 percent of the girls stated that they felt the school had in some way indicated the desirability of continuing education beyond the high school.

More than one-half (54.7 percent) of the youths knew of no scholarships that might have been available to them. Seven in ten of the youths and almost eight in ten of the parents knew of no resources in the local community that might provide some financial assistance in helping the youths continue education beyond the high school. Six in ten of the youths had not talked with a college representative about the possibilities of continuing their education.

In 34.7 percent of the cases, the youths themselves indicated that finances were a factor in their failure to continue education beyond the high school. Parents reported that in 46.6 percent of the cases finances were a factor, and the school officials reported that in 49.5 percent (433) of the cases they were a great factor. The four readers considered finances as first or second most important factors in the failure of 38.9 percent of the boys and 30.0 percent of the girls to continue their education.

In considering the opinions of the youths, their parents, the school officials, and the readers, it seems safe to say that approximately 35 to 50 percent of the youths found finances to be a major contributing factor in their failure to continue with education beyond the high school.

As for marriage, 67.5 percent of the girls and 37.3 percent of the boys were either married or planning to be married soon. The four readers indicated that marriage was the reason of first or second importance for 46.4 percent of the girls and 13.0 percent of the boys.

When asked whether the attitude of their parents was unfavorable toward further education, 24.1 percent of the girls and 15.3 percent of the boys said that it was. The parents agreed fairly closely with them, as 27.9 percent of the parents of the girls and 16.5 percent of those of the boys indicated that they did not want the youths to continue. In the opinion of the school officials, however, parental attitude toward further education acted to hinder the youths in continuing their education in 41.7 percent of the cases. The four readers considered "parental opposition or indifference" as a real cause (first or second choice) for 16.4 percent of the girls and 12.3 percent of the boys.

Reports from 55.9 percent of the boys and 43.4 percent of the girls indicated they really did want to continue their education; however, in the opinion of the school officials, approximately eight in ten youths had left the impression, in one way or another, that they did not want to continue.

A majority of the youths (54.9 percent) decided not to continue their education some time during the senior year in high school.

The four review readers indicated that the attitudes of those youth who regarded the high school as terminal, who desired to start earning immediately, or who had some other interest were a major factor affecting their decision not to continue for 58.7 percent of the boys and 35.4 percent of the girls. The four readers also indicated that indifference was a real obstacle in the case of 43.3 percent of the girls and 35.6 percent of the boys. In more than one-half of the cases, the close friends of the youths did not continue their education beyond the high school.

In regard to the distance of a college or university from the homes of these students, it was found that 63.3 percent of the youths lived within 20 miles of a college or university; another 28.9 percent lived within 21 to 40 miles; and 5.1 percent lived more than 40 miles from an institution of higher learning. Only 13.3 percent of the youths stated that they would have continued their education if they could have lived at home while attending school, while the parents of 11.4 percent of the youths thought that the youths would have continued their education if there had been a college or university in the local community.

Two other phases of this study were: (1) to sample the next 10 percent of high school graduating classes to determine if the reasons given by students in the upper 10 percent of graduating classes for not continuing higher education were any different from those we would have obtained had we included the upper 20 percent of the graduating classes, and (2) to determine what differences there might be between paired cases of those who did go to college and those who did not.

The sample of the *additional* 10 percent of the graduating class gave no indication of any variance with the reasons given by the larger study of the upper 10 percent only. It would be fair to say from our sampling that, had the study included the upper 20 percent instead of the upper 10 percent, the reasons and conditions given for not continuing their education would have shown no significant difference.

The second continuation of the study was done by matching in the upper 10 percent in the same graduating class of 1955 one who went to college and one who did not. These were studied by individual interviews. They were in reality matched in three ways: (1) They were from the same high school class; (2) They were in the same decile (upper 10 percent) of the same class; (3) They were matched by sex. Of the total number, we were able to match completely only 141 cases.

There are some significant differences in these two matched

groups. Of those who went to college, approximately 7 percent said that loans would be necessary, 55 percent expected to or had gotten scholarship help, 78 percent said they expected to help by their own employment. However, 92 percent of the students said they were being financed to a greater or lesser degree by their parents. This in itself would indicate that funds beyond those coming from parents would be used to supplement the cost of their continued education in a large number of the cases.

Then the two groups were matched and reported by the parents. The question asked of the parents of those who continued was "Is it necessary that some financial assistance be made available to this student from sources outside the immediate family— such as scholarships, loans, and student employment?" *Yes,* 61 percent; *No,* 39 percent. The question asked the parents of those not continuing was, "Was his (or her) not continuing a matter of money?" *Yes,* 64.6 percent; *No,* 35.4 percent. The interesting point here is that nearly the same percentage of parents in both groups indicated that there must be some additional financial help beyond the immediate family. Of those students who went, 39 percent would evidently be entirely supported by the family; however, of those who did not go, 35 percent of the parents said that continuing was not a matter of money. It seems apparent that those who do go are having problems of money also and that at least 35 percent of those who did not continue would have been in financial position to do so.

The annual income of parents shows a difference in favor of those who continued their education:

Family Income	Percentage Who Did Continue	Percentage Who Did Not Continue
Income $5,000 or below..............	34	65
Income above $5,000...............	66	35

The time at which the decision was made to continue or discontinue education beyond the high school showed a marked difference:

Decision Made In	Percentage Who Decided To Continue	Percentage Who Decided Not To Continue
Ninth grade.......................	61.0	3.6
Tenth grade.......................	7.8	3.6
Eleventh grade....................	12.1	8.5
Twelfth grade.....................	15.6	47.5
Other, or did not know.............	3.5	38.9

It is apparent that a rather large percentage of those who planned to continue their education beyond the high school came to that decision very early in their high school years. Of those who did not continue, 47.5 percent did not decide finally until their senior year of high school. This early decision to continue is probably indicative of early and continued interest and motivation to continue education. More than half of those who did not continue seemed to have reached that decision at an early date also. Those who had decided not to continue under the heading "Other, or did not know" had for the most part never considered continuing their education beyond the high school.

The educational level of the parents of those who continued and those who did not continue showed differences in favor of those who continued:

	EDUCATIONAL LEVEL ATTAINED BY PARENT		
	Median Grade Attained	Attended College (%)	Completed College (%)
Youth who did continue			
Father	12	34.0	20.6
Mother	12	30.0	9.9
Youth who did not continue			
Father	10	8.4	1.4
Mother	10	7.7	3.5

This would indicate that the grade level attained by parents of those continuing was approximately two years above that of the parents of those not continuing. It is also interesting to note that 39 percent of the parents of those who did not continue had reached only the eighth grade as their highest grade level while only 16 percent of the parents of those who did continue had reached that grade only. It is fair to conclude that the parental background of those who continued was superior to that of those who did not continue.

We have had some interest in the proximity of a college to the local community. Of the students who did continue school, approximately 24 percent were attending in their home community, and 76 percent were attending a school outside the home community. When the question was asked of the other group of parents, "Do you think he would have continued if there had been a school in his community?" the answers were as follows: *Yes,* 27.7 percent; *No,* 72.3 percent. This with other evidence we have from two other studies in Indiana gives continuing evidence that approximately 25 percent will go to a college in their own community and 75 percent will go outside their own community. This may change in the future, but it has been a surprisingly constant figure for a long time in our state of Indiana.

Other differences in favor of those continuing as against those not continuing may be roughly noted as they were reported by school officials, parents, and students of these two groups:

1. Parental attitude was stronger toward more schooling for those continuing.
2. Somewhat larger group of close friends also continued.
3. Students' attitudes toward high school work were better.
4. A larger percentage of parents wanted them to continue.
5. All those who continued really wanted to continue.
6. College representatives talked with twice as many who continued as those who did not. In fact, 57 percent of those who did not continue talked to no college representative.
7. Students who continued were much more aware of community help and scholarship opportunity than those who did not.
8. A small percentage of those who continued had plans for marriage or were married, while 54 percent of those who did not continue were married or had immediate plans.
9. All those who continued had made plans whereas approximately 60 percent of those who did not continue had (according to parents) made no plans for continuing.

Like the original study, this study seems to emphasize two factors: lack of motivation and money are the major factors for good high school students not continuing their education beyond the high school. It is difficult to differentiate these factors because they are often intermingled. However, my belief is that lack of personal incentive is a marked factor.

Summary of Reports on College-Going Plans of High School Students

ROBERT E. IFFERT

Chief, Faculty and Student Services, Office of Education,
Department of Health, Education, and Welfare

IT WOULD BE PRESUMPTUOUS AND FUTILE FOR ME TO ATTEMPT TO summarize orally what these gentlemen have reported, so I have prepared a handout (see Table 2). I understand that is something that is always expected of a government person. I have to apologize to the panel members for taking the liberty of putting into such brief form what they have done in many hours of hard work. I must also ask their forgiveness for taking liberty with their terminology.

One thing that has been pointed out very clearly this morning in these discussions has been the fact that we face a difficult job of determining the percentage from each tenth of our high school graduates who go to college. One reason grows out of the fact that more boys than girls go to college and more girls than boys stand in the upper tenth or the top tenth of high school classes. This anomalous situation immediately introduces a problem.

A few years ago, in cooperation with the American Association of Collegiate Registrars and Admissions Officers, the Office of Education conducted a study of dropouts in which 147 colleges participated. The numbers and percentages of students who were in each tenth of their high school class were reported. From the records of the more than 12,000 students in this study it would appear that between 71 and 72 percent of the highest tenth of high school graduates were continuing their education on a full-time basis. We were doing the same thing as Dean Wright. We counted the nursing schools, business colleges, any education beyond the high school as continuing education, and on the basis of those figures, it appeared that 32 percent of all high school

TABLE 2.—SUMMARY OF RECENT REPORTS ON COLLEGE-GOING PLANS OF HIGH SCHOOL STUDENTS

IDENTIFICATION OF REPORT	PERCENT OF STUDENTS EXPRESSING EACH ATTITUDE OR ASPIRATION WITH REFERENCE TO COLLEGE ATTENDANCE, BY SEX									PERCENT OF TOTAL WHO DID ATTEND		
	Positive			Negative			Uncertain or Indifferent					
	Total	Men	Women	Total	Men	Women	Total	Men	Women	Total	Men	Women
Berdie* (1954)	40	45	36	60	55	64	—	—	—	—	—	—
Daughtry† (1956)	46	62	33	—	—	—	16	12	20	40	46	34
ETS=NSF‡ (1956)	70	78	62	14	10	18	16	12	20	—	—	—
Slocum§ (1956)	36	38	35	42	36	47	22	26	18	—	—	—
ETS=NSF‖ (1957)	50	56	44	27	23	30	23	21	26	36	42	30
Industrial Foundation** (1958)	52	—	—	31	—	—	17	—	—	39	—	—
Little†† (1958)	45	43	47	43	34	52	12	23	1	—	—	—
Stroup and Andrew‡‡ (1958)	45	51	39	55	49	61	—	—	—	26	30	22
Wright and Jung§§ (1959)	—	—	—	—	—	—	—	—	—	71	85	64

* Ralph F. Berdie, *After High School—What?* (Minneapolis: University of Minnesota Press, 1954).

† Alex A. Daughtry, *A Report on the Post-Graduation Activities of the 1955 Kansas High School Graduates* (Emporia: Kansas State Teachers College, 1956).

‡ Glen Stice, William Mollenkopf, and Warren S. Torgerson, *Background Factors and College-Going Plans among High-Aptitude Public High School Seniors* (Princeton, N.J.: Educational Testing Service, 1956).

§ W. L. Slocum, *Occupational and Educational Plans of High School Seniors from Farm and Non-Farm Homes,* Bulletin 564, Institute of Agricultural Sciences, State College of Washington (Pullman: The College, 1956).

‖ *Background Factors Relating to College Plans & College Enrollment among Public High School Students* (Princeton, N.J.: Educational Testing Service, 1957).

** Industrial Foundation on Education, *The Case for Increasing Student Motivation* (Toronto, Ont.: The Foundation, 1958).

†† J. Kenneth Little, "A State Wide Inquiry into Decisions of Youth about Education beyond High School" (Unpublished research report, School of Education, University of Wisconsin, September 1958).

‡‡ Francis Stroup and Dean C. Andrew, "Barriers to College Attendance" (MS filed with the U.S. Office of Education, 1958).

§§ Wendell W. Wright and Christian Jung, "Why Capable High School Students Do Not Continue Their Schooling," Bulletin, School of Education, Indiana University, Vol. XXXV, No. 1, January 1959 (Bloomington: Division of Research and Field Services, Indiana University, 1959).

75

graduates were continuing with their education. That is low in terms of present figures. The percentage is up now. It would appear from the statistics of the Office of Education showing the number of first-time entrants and the number of high school graduates that nearly 50 percent of high school graduates enter college, either on a full-time or part-time basis.

In this connection I would like to point to a publication of the Industrial Foundation on Education, of Toronto, Canada, which bears out what Dean Wright was saying to the effect that possibly we aren't doing so badly. I will read two paragraphs from this publication which is entitled *The Case for Increasing Student Motivation:*

> The United States enrolls about 3 million students in post-secondary schools. This is about 30 per cent of the 18–21 year age group. This figure has to be modified by several facts; a number of the people enrolled fall outside the 18 to 21 age group; probably a significant number are not intellectually qualified to succeed in the field of education they have chosen and will become "drop-outs."
>
> Even with these modifications, however, it is apparent that, in the United States, a very large proportion of those qualified to proceed with their education beyond the secondary school are, in fact doing so, and something close to 30 per cent is not an unreasonable figure.

The Industrial Foundation was searching for an answer to the question, "How many have the potential to take higher education?" They estimate that both in Russia and in the United States more than 30 percent of the respective college-age groups are in post-secondary education. There follows the conclusion that, "It is not unreasonable to expect that over 30 percent of a given age group is capable of benefiting from a post-secondary school education."

I hope that some of our people who go to Russia and come back with high acclaim for their educational system are as much mistaken about how well the Russians are doing as some of our Canadian friends are about how well we are doing. We certainly are not getting our 30 percent exclusively from the top levels of intellectual ability.

There is one point that Mr. Daughtry made which I would like to comment on. He referred to the question of the validity of the response when it was made in a local situation. In the Office of Education we are making a more intensive follow-up study of 20 of the 147 institutions selected from the earlier study of dropouts. In the first study the students reported the more personal items of information directly to the Office rather than through the college. In the present study they are reporting directly to the college on items about family income, reasons for certain actions such as dropping out for disciplinary reasons or for academic deficiencies, and so forth. It is rather interesting that in these same institutions we seem to have received much franker responses from the students when they were made directly to an impersonal agency rather than back to the college. Personal status seems to be involved. They hesitate to give such information as freely and possibly as accurately in some situations. I suggest that if you sometimes find discrepancies among studies you may also find differences in method. If the responses were made under conditions in which some of these sociological and psychological factors played an important part, results would obviously be different.

Dean Wright mentioned, in connection with the reports on financial needs, the high percentage of their college-bound students who were also from homes of fairly well-educated parents. This points to the need for further research. It would be interesting to know, for example, how many of the Merit Scholarship awardees, or grantees, are sons and daughters of parents who had gone to college; how much of the financial aid is being given in the form of scholarships to people who would go to college anyway; and how much of it is going to assist those who would not otherwise be able to go.

Discussion Following Panel Statements

Presiding: WENDELL W. WRIGHT

CHAIRMAN WRIGHT: We are ready for discussion. When you raise a question, I shall try to refer it to the appropriate person.

MR. SCHREIBER: Kenneth Little said that the children who did go on to college never thought that they would not go to college. The implication of this statement for the public school people is that they must create in the mind of the child very early that college is in his future.

I would like to recount an incident that happened to one of our third-grade children. The class had been discussing a topic in science. One child kept on asking more and more probing questions. The teacher, who had answered him as best she could, finally said, "You will learn more about this topic when you get to junior high school, high school, and college." The youngster popped up and said, "College? Who, me? College is not for me, that's for rich people." We have to overcome the attitude that college is only for the rich.

Now, the question I would like to ask of any one of the four gentlemen is this: Richard King, of the Harvard admissions office, has stated that the *mother's* educational level seems to be a better indicator of the child's future educational goal than the father's. All I have heard so far from you, Gentlemen, deals with the father's background, the father's income, and, once in a while, "the parents'." Has any study been done by any of you on the *mother's* educational level as it relates to the child's goal?

CHAIRMAN WRIGHT: May I undertake to report on this one. I happen to have the data before me. Only 8 percent of the mothers whose children did not go to college went to college themselves, whereas 30 percent of mothers whose children did go to college went to college themselves. Moreover, only 3.5 percent of the mothers in the first group completed college whereas 10 percent in the second group did so.

DR. LITTLE: We collected some information on this point, but we didn't follow through with it completely. In the main, the education of the mothers and of the fathers were so much alike that we called it the education of the parents.

In a little substudy, we tried to appraise the effect of parents having attended college. In Wisconsin, one-half of the parents of high school graduates were not themselves high school graduates, and one-third of them had not even attended high school.

About 10 percent had attended college, and about 9 percent were college graduates. That was the state picture for parents.

We then studied the children of these groups of parents. If neither parent had attended college, only about 20 percent of the children went to college. If one parent had attended college, this was closer to 40 percent. If both parents attended college, this was closer to 75 percent.

When we looked at the difference in education of the father and mother, we found a higher percentage of the children going to college if the mother had attended college than if only the father had attended college. This was not a great difference, however. Whether it was really significant, I can't say, but the trend was in that direction.

Dr. Stroup: We found that the mother's background seemed to influence college attendance more than the father's, particularly if the mother had ever been a teacher. If the mother had ever taught, the chances were greatly enhanced in favor of the child going to college.

Raymond C. Hummel (Assistant Professor of Education, Graduate School of Education, Harvard University): This question can become more complex. Charles McArthur studied a group of selected students at Harvard and found that the influence of parental education is affected, in turn, by other factors. For example, he divided the group into upper, middle, and lower socioeconomic classes; then he attempted to find out who exercised the power in the family, that is, who "wore the pants" in terms of making the operational decisions. Finally, he tried to determine whether the boy was defensive in his relationship with the dominant parent or whether he accepted this parent's authority.

When he obtained all this information, he was able to make some very interesting predictions, not concerning the field of choice, but as to whether this boy would move on to become an upper-level or a run-of-the-mill physician, whether this boy was potentially upper-level corporate management or middle-level. This shows how complex the question may be. The mere incidence of parental education does not answer this kind of question.

DR. BRIERLY: I am a little bit concerned about the results that were derived from questionnaires without personal interviews. I am inclined to question the data suggesting that financial difficulty is the reason why most students do not go to college; likewise, I question the data suggesting that these students really hope to get some future education in some way. I think one would normally expect about three-fourths of the people to write back that they could not afford to go to college and that they hope to continue their education some day.

I think these responses are too obvious and, in many cases, conceal the real reasons for not going to college. The easiest thing in the world to say is that you can't afford to go and that you certainly hope to go later. But what do these responses really mean? In the study in which you had personal interviews with the students and tried to get beneath their general statements and appraise them, there are no doubt valid results. I question the results of the others. These are just the answers that you would expect to receive from questionnaires.

CHAIRMAN WRIGHT: When our interviewer went to one home (and I remember his telling me about this exceptional case), he had to go out to a lake to see the family. There he found a couple of speedboats, a Cadillac, and so forth; yet, he was told that the family couldn't afford to send the girl to college! He didn't accept that reason for the report, of course.

DR. STROUP: With all that to keep up, I don't see how they could afford to send the girl to college!

DR. LITTLE: I would like to respond to that. Some of the material I considered bringing here describes the personal reasons students gave for not going to college after high school and for dropping out of college if they did go. The responses that interested me were not the ones that cited financial difficulties. In most cases, these were obviously true. The ones that interested me were ones that cited preferences for things other than education.

ANN TANNEYHILL (Director of Vocational Services, National Urban League): I hope that during our discussions we will not lose sight of three things: The first is that many of these young people are disadvantaged even before they cross the threshold of primary school. The second is that these disadvantaged children, especially in minority groups, do not have an image of themselves currently or of themselves as adults that motivates them at all. And the third is that this self-image cannot be changed in many instances without the cooperation of the parents.

I wonder if we can't come up with some suggestions for research that will lead to action programs so that institutions of higher education in cooperation with the public school and the community agencies will be able to do something about these problems.

FLORENCE C. MYERS (Administrative Assistant in Charge of Guidance, George Washington High School, New York City): Our school is involved with Junior High School 43 in the experiment to upgrade potentially able students, and I want to underscore what Miss Tanneyhill just said about the importance of giving these young people from disadvantaged areas a feeling of self-respect. Many of them (not all of them) are victims of neglect and rejection at home, and one of the first responsibilities of the guidance counselors and of the instructional staff is to make these young people realize that they have something to give, that they are important, and that they are recognized.

To many of them, college is associated with people who have money and who can afford to go. We provide a long orientation focusing on self-assessment and self-evaluation. We do everything we can do to make them feel that they are important, contributing members of the school community. A very important factor in this whole program of upgrading and developing potentially able students in deprived areas is to give them a tremendous amount of individual attention. This cannot be done without an increase in the number of instructors and an increase in the number of guidance counselors. Any school that attempts to introduce a program of this kind without increasing personnel will have a very difficult time. Another important factor is that the entire school must understand the objectives and become involved in this total program.

RICHARD L. PLAUT (President, National Scholarship Service and Fund for Negro Students): I want to make one observation on the studies that have been reported. I think it is worth noting that all of them seem to be largely concerned with what I like to call the academic survivor, that is, the youngster who reaches the twelfth grade with college qualifications. Our greatest loss of potential talent comes from high school dropouts and those who reach the twelfth grade without college qualifications.

DR. LITTLE: At the time our study began, the university also established the guidance laboratory for superior students. The guidance workers at this laboratory are cooperating with the high schools to identify the talented youngsters, to bring them in for conference and discussion, and to widen their horizons. The laboratory has more business than it can accomplish. It endeavors to improve the counseling programs in the high schools and bring counselors in to observe the students. So there is an action program going along hand-in-hand with the fact-finding program.

DR. WOLFLE: Did any of you take account of the large amount of geographic mobility, or did you follow only those students who stayed in the state? I have two possible effects in mind: (1) a distortion of the statistics; (2) the effect on the student. Did any of you try to find out through samples what the geographic mobility does to disturb these figures and whether it is associated with falling off the educational ladder?

CHAIRMAN WRIGHT: In our study, we found that 17 percent of the students went to colleges outside the state. Frankly, it was just a matter of distance that kept us from trying to follow them. Miami University happens to be just across the state line; so we could follow up on those students rather easily. Some went to Minnesota, and I didn't want to go there in the wintertime; some went to Florida, and I didn't have money enough to go there! By and large, though, we did not attempt to follow them outside the state, simply because of the circumstances.

DR. LITTLE: In our study, we followed them wherever they went, and we found that the persistence of those who went outside the state was not greatly different from those who remained in the state.

DR. STROUP: We found the same thing. A slightly higher number of the more talented students went outside the state.

DR. WOLFLE: There is the more difficult problem of what this moving about does to students prior to twelfth grade; what are the losses that occur along the road?

DR. STICE: I have a little information on that. We haven't looked at it in detail. It appears, however, that a good deal of the attrition between the tenth and twelfth grades results not from the student dropping out of school but from moving. Very often the school in which the student had been registered in tenth grade reported that he had left school and requested a transfer to some other school. From the Midwest they seemed to move often to California. Californians, of course, stay in California. When we tried to follow these students through the school to which a transcript had been sent, we found that the student didn't arrive, had never been heard of, or stayed only a couple of weeks. Some moved to a third school or even a fourth, but most of them seemed to quit by the process of transfer. On the other hand, there does not seem to be quite as much moving by families with children in this age-range as there is among families in general.

DR. THEOBALD: I wonder if any studies have been made to see how neighborhood and community attitudes influence school attendance and persistence. It seems to me that community attitudes toward school often override the other factors in importance. For example, if you made a study in the New York City colleges, you would probably get a completely different picture from the one you get in the Midwestern communities. In New York, I think you would find that only 6 or 7 percent of the students come from college homes. What are the differences in two communities that result in such different patterns? There must be a crucial difference in the attitudes toward education. I think we have to ask more than "Did the father or mother go to college?"

DR. LITTLE: We found high-income areas with a low yield of college-going students and, conversely, low-income communities with high yields. Just as you have indicated, we found that community attitudes and parental encouragement were crucial. In some instances, we could trace it back to ethnic backgrounds. We found two communities of about the same size and general characteristics. Almost twice as many students were going to college from one as from the other. The extent to which the parents were encouraging them was just about in that ratio. The background in the low-yield community was rural, German and Polish; the background in the other community was rural and Scandinavian. And we found this rather consistent throughout our state: that wherever we could locate rural Polish communities, it was a low-yield community; that wherever we found rural Scandinavian communities, it was a high-yield community. The differences between the communities narrowed, however, when we came to the most able students.

SISTER COLUMBA, S.N.D. (Academic Vice-President, Trinity College, Washington, D.C.): Did you make any comparison between the teachers in the high-yield and low-yield communities to see if there was any difference in the encouragement they gave to their students?

DR. LITTLE: The students reported whether or not they discussed their plans with the teachers, and if so, whether this had much influence. The results showed that they did discuss their plans with teachers but that they attributed more influence to their parents. They did not, in general, attribute much influence to their teachers; however, in a few instances, they did cite the encouragement of an individual teacher as an important factor.

REXFORD G. MOON, JR. (Director of the College Scholarship Service, College Entrance Examination Board): There are some interesting studies being conducted on the effect which the peer group has on the individual's plans for higher education. James Coleman of Johns Hopkins and others have done and are continuing to do some very interesting community studies along these lines. These studies are particularly interesting because they emphasize the tremendous influence which the peer group has upon the individual's incentives.

CHAIRMAN WRIGHT: We have exceeded our time limit. The discussion has been interesting and informative, but we must now adjourn.

Group Membership and Higher Education

RALPH F. BERDIE

Director, Student Counseling Bureau,
University of Minnesota

SOMETIMES THE RESEARCH AND DISCUSSION WE DIRECT TOWARD social and educational problems attains so much intrinsic interest that we tend to forget our purposes for studying the phenomena which concern us. When we study the differences in personal incentive for higher education among various social groups, we run the risk of becoming so intrigued by the large and significant differences that can easily be identified that we may forget why our attention was called to the problem in the first place. Let us devote a few minutes to the question of why we wish to know how group membership is related to matriculation proclivity, to coin a new phrase.

Perhaps some small portion of interest in this problem comes solely from our curiosity about human behavior. Many of us assume that college attendance, like other aspects of human behavior, can be explained by recourse to psychological and social principles. Our interest in the problem is not much different qualitatively from our interest in a rat who runs a maze or a college sophomore who learns to withdraw his finger from an electric shock in a conditioning experiment. I believe, however, that this type of motivation is not the primary one for most of us when we study problems of college attendance.

The second purpose underlying this study is the hope that our new information will lead to an increased probability that any student who can benefit from higher education will have the opportunity to have this experience, and that society as a whole will gain from the resulting increase in the number of well-educated individuals. Our primary purpose in studying the relationship between group membership and college attendance is an admittedly practical one. We hope to be able to change the behavior of a large number of individuals in the direction that we as educators, committed to the importance of our role, deem valuable and desirable.

The research that you heard described this morning has already emphasized for you, and the research that will be presented this afternoon again will emphasize, that children of wealthy families seek higher education more frequently than do children of poorer families, that more white children go to college than do nonwhite, that boys go to college more than girls, and that metropolitan children go to college more often than do rural children. This kind of information is helpful, and in fact is necessary, if we are to learn more about personal incentive for higher education, if we are to discover ways of developing social programs to achieve our ends, and if we are to learn how to work effectively with individual students who should be encouraged to seek higher education. I believe that this kind of information that we have been collecting so energetically during the past decade is most necessary, and I have done my share in attempting to accumulate and understand statistics and frequencies. By this time, however, a great deal of this information has been collected by a number of persons from a number of geographical areas, and the question well might be raised, "What are the next steps?"

We have heard of the studies that have been done in a variety of states by a number of persons, and also of the fewer number of studies that have been done on a national basis. Private individuals, state universities, and governmental bureaus have accumulated a vast number of figures, and effective work has been done in synthesizing and interpreting these data. Very seldom are contradictory facts uncovered, and, in general, one study tends to confirm and extend the generalizations that have been made by previous studies. On the whole, the information we now have concerning the college-going behavior of individuals comprising various social groups is well established and well buttressed with facts.

Where do we go now? We have not reached the time when we can cease our search for new facts, but certainly we have arrived at a point in time when we can take the facts we have and use them in developing programs that will result in larger numbers of competent individuals attending college.

The information we already have suggests that certain groups merit special attention and that special programs well might be directed toward these groups. For instance, high-ability children coming from families of low economic status require special attention and efforts, as do children coming from certain racial groups, and from certain religious groups, and from certain geographical areas. If the information we have already does not allow us to use a rifle instead of a shotgun, at least it allows us to scatter our shots over a somewhat smaller area.

The type of social program that has received most attention is that related to scholarships. The relationship between economic status and college attendance is easily observed, and the application of money to the place that hurts is an accepted treatment. No other types of social programs have been widely used. Why has no one attempted systematically to use the resources found in the PTA, libraries, and the farm Grange? Why don't colleges and states have agents to talk to parents of talented children coming from the non-college-going groups? Why are not greater attempts made to introduce magazines, books, and newspapers into the homes of these pupils in the hope that even symptomatic treatments sometimes work? Why don't we use some imagination?

The information we have about the behavior of groups does not aid us particularly in explaining the behavior of an individual. For instance, we know that relatively more boys attend college than do girls; at least this is true in Minnesota. We also know, again at least in Minnesota, that more metropolitan and urban children attend college than do rural children. On the other hand, we also know that more girls from farms attend college than do boys. We know that more children from upper-income families attend college than from lower-income families. In certain areas of Minnesota, however, more children from lower-income families attend college than from higher-income families. And this relationship between income and college attendance is different in these areas for the sexes. Thus, if we know something about a given group to which the individual belongs, we can make some predictions with known probabilities of college attendance. However, if we know that a single individual is a member of two given groups, we can make a prediction which may be quite different from the prediction made on the basis of more restricted information, but yet which may be a prediction with a higher level of probability. Thus, the more we know about the behavior of various groups with which the individual can be identified, the more likely we are to predict correctly the person's behavior. The information we already have allows us to reduce our errors of prediction to some extent, but this information which for the most part has been gained through the study of frequency statistics derived from groups does little to allow us to change the predicted behavior of any one given individual.

Let me cite an example. We know that in Minnesota boys coming from upper-income farm families whose background is German and Catholic and who live in the southern part of the state are less likely to attend college than boys who come from low-economic farm families of Finnish Protestant background in the northern part of the state. When we interviewed two of the boys from the first group, that is, from the group not planning college, we found that one of these boys started to work with his father on the family farm at a very early age, that by the age of fourteen he was managing two hundred acres that his father had rented from an adjoining farm, and that at graduation the father was planning to give this land to his son so that the son could continue to farm it. The second boy from this same group had very little experience working with his father on the farm but for several years had found school dull and uninteresting. The family had only one book in its home, a Bible, and the only literature that came to the house was mail-order catalogues and the weekly newspaper. The father and mother worked hard throughout the entire day, and the family retired early in the evening, night after night. The farm was relatively isolated and the boy had little opportunity to associate with other children. His interest in farming, which was not great, by far exceeded his interest in school, and at an early age he had decided to terminate his formal education as soon as possible. Thus, both of these boys who were equally bright and who had enough ability to do college work, and who behaved according to the prediction that would have been made on the basis of their group memberships, fulfilled these predictions for different reasons. In the first case the boy had a strong incentive for something other than college, and in the second, education had a negative valence instead of a positive one.

Let me give you another example. Two very bright boys in a metropolitan high school came from families of similar economic status. The parents of neither boy had completed more than the tenth grade, and the family income in both instances always had been marginal. The boys lived in the same neighborhood, they seemed to have the same cultural backgrounds, and very little difference could be seen between the two. One of the boys was planning to attend college; the other was not. The second boy explained to his counselor that, already as a high school senior, he had far more education than anybody else in the family and that when he moved into a skilled trade, as he planned, he would be moving up the occupational ladder several steps, as the other persons in the family were all employed at unskilled jobs. The other boy explained to the counselor that he planned to attend college as a result of two visits to his family made by his mother's cousin who was a college graduate and a successful accountant. These two visits, and the discussions and attitudes related to them, apparently, had influenced the boy and his family enough so that his college plans were affected.

The point I am trying to make is that the group differences we observe do little in themselves *to explain* the behavior of the individual. Children from low-income families do not fail to attend college simply because they belong to this group but rather because a number of conditions are associated with low incomes—restricted educational and cultural experiences in the family, association with others not attending college, occupational goals which do not involve college training, and similar conditions. Girls do not fail to attend college simply because they are girls, but rather because of a number of conditions related to femininity—parental attitudes toward the education of women, the types of education provided for women by many coeducational institutions, attitudes of men toward the education of wives, and such. Catholicism as such does not discourage higher education; look at the support the church gives to it. But conditions related to Catholicism are related to college nonattendance, and Catholics may wonder if they should not have incentive programs particularly appropriate for their groups.

Some clues about these kinds of conditions can be derived through studies of group differences similar to some we have done in Minnesota. For instance, we identified a group of high-ability boys coming from the homes of skilled laborers and then compared the group planning to attend college with the group having no such plans, on a number of variables. We found here for instance that the education of the mother was an important differential. We then could have taken a group of high-ability boys from the homes of skilled laborers where the mother had been a high school graduate and again divided the group into those who were and those who were not going to college and made comparison. This kind of analysis can be carried on indefinitely; only experience can tell us where to stop. Methods of partial correlation may be useful here. Equally productive, however, will be the more intensive case study of students planning to attend various types of colleges and students having no such plans.

Regardless of how much we know about groups of students, we always will have to have specific information about the individual students who concern us, and, if we are to provide incentive to individuals, regardless of the groups to which they belong, we must have someone who can gain an understanding of each individual, learn of his needs and capacities, and then with ingenuity and imagination discover how that person's incentive for higher education can be made effective.

Encouraging Personal Incentive for Higher Education among Youth from Low-Income Groups

ROBERT J. HAVIGHURST

Professor of Education, University of Chicago

THE PAST DECADE HAS SEEN A REMARKABLE INCREASE IN THE proportion of youth from lower-income families who have gone to college. Table 3 gives an overview of the percentages of youth from the various social class groups who have entered college since 1920. Whereas the proportion of upper- and upper-middle-class boys entering college has doubled since 1920, the proportion of lower-middle-class boys has quintupled, and the proportion of upper-lower-class boys has multiplied by ten.

At present about 40 percent of boys enter college, and about 27 percent of girls. Clearly, in the case of boys we are getting close to the limit, if we think of the upper half in terms of intelligence as being good material for college. As Table 4 shows, only about 16 percent of the boys are in the upper half of the group in intelligence and not in college. The great majority of these boys come from working-class homes or their fathers have small white-collar jobs. They are the ones who lack personal incentive for higher education, generally complicated by lack of money.

In the River City cohort, whose progress the writer and his colleagues studied from the time its members were in the sixth grade until some of them went to college, there were 53 boys in the top quartile of intellectual ability. Thirty-four went to college. The 19 able non-college boys came mainly from working-class homes, had average or below average school grades, had a lower achievement drive than the college-going boys, and lower personality adjustment scores than college-goers. Five of them did not graduate from high school. This presents the problem in a nutshell. Why do these able boys not go to college?

TABLE 3.—PERCENT OF YOUTH ENTERING COLLEGE, BY SOCIAL CLASS

SOCIAL CLASS	PERCENT OF TOTAL YOUTH POPULATION	PERCENT OF YOUTH ENTERING COLLEGE						
		U.S. 1920* (Estimates)	U.S. 1940* (Estimates)	1948, Boston, Males	1958, River City		U.S. 1960* (Estimates)	
					Males	Females	Males	Females
Upper and Upper Middle..	10	40	80	80	75	70	85	70
Lower Middle..	30	10	20	50	45	32	55	35
Upper Lower...	40	2	5	15	20	17	25	18
Lower Lower...	20	0	0	6	6	0	10	5

* Figures are the author's estimates for the United States.
SOURCES.—*Boston:* Adapted from Joseph A. Kahl, "Education and Occupational Aspirations of 'Common Man' Boys," *Harvard Educational Review*, XXIII (1953), 186–203.
River City: From data gathered by the writer and his colleagues for a forthcoming book entitled *Growing Up in River City.*

TABLE 4.—INTELLECTUAL ABILITY AND COLLEGE ENTRANCE, 1960

| QUARTILE FOR SCHOLASTIC APTITUDE | PERCENTAGES OF YOUTH POPULATION | | | |
| | Enter College | | Do Not Enter College | |
	Male	Female	Male	Female
I (high)................	19	14	6	11
II.....................	15	9	10	16
III....................	4	3	21	22
IV.....................	2	1	23	24

Why Able Students Do Not Attend College

There are three general reasons why able students may not go to college. These will be discussed, one by one.

1. *Finances.* The purely economic reason of lack of money has been shown in several studies to be less important than lack of motivation in preventing able young people from going to college. Money is necessary but is not sufficient to get and to keep an able student in college. With the current relatively favorable scholarship and loan provisions, and the tradition of student employment, the financial barrier is not insurmountable.

2. *Propinquity.* There is a tendency toward a greater amount of college attendance in communities with a local college than in communities distant from a college. However, colleges are so widely available that relatively few young people live beyond commuting distance from a college. Those who are distant from a college have this disadvantage, but it is not a great one.

3. *Motivation.* The personal incentive for a college education arises from the following factors:

   a) Need or drive for achievement.
   b) Identification with a person or persons who have gone to college.
   c) Social pressure.
   d) Intrinsic pleasure in learning.

This theory of motivation for college has been worked out and tried out by the author and his colleagues, and found to apply quite well to the boys in the River City study.[1]

a) Need for achievement.—As a measure of the basic need for achievement, Stivers used the test developed by McClelland, a form of "thematic apperception test" in which students looked at pictures showing young men in situations where they might be undertaking some task, and then wrote brief stories on what they thought the young men were doing. For instance, a picture might show a young man in a white coat standing before a desk and holding a small object up in front of him. This might be seen as a chemist analyzing a substance, or a man studying to be a doctor, or any of a number of other things. The story is scored on the basis of the kind of ideas and the number of them which deal with achievement of a goal, of striving to succeed, and getting ahead in the world. This need for achievement is a deep and possibly unconscious drive of which a person may not be fully aware. Consequently it is necessary to measure it by some indirect method, such as the McClelland test.

Stivers found that the boys who were well motivated for college had a higher need for achievement than those who were not motivated for college.

b) Identification with persons who have gone to college.—Students were asked which adults had been most influential in their lives. It was found that those who were most desirous of going to college had more parents or close relatives or teachers and other "significant persons" who had gone to college or had urged them to go to college.

c) Social pressure.—In an interview, a student was asked what people and what agencies set college as a desirable goal for him —family, schoolteachers, age-mates, community leaders, books, and so forth. The interview was scored on the basis of the number of these influences which were favorable toward going to

---

[1] See Eugene H. Stivers, "Motivation for College in High School Boys," *School Review*, LXVI (1958), 341–50, and "Motivation for College in High School Girls," *School Review*, LXVII (1959), 320–34; Bernard C. Rosen and Roy D'Andrade, "The Psychosocial Origins of Achievement Motivation," *Sociometry*, XXII (1959), 185–218; David C. McClelland, *et al.*, *The Achievement Motive* (New York: Appleton-Century-Crofts, 1953); David C. McClelland, *et al.*, *Talent and Society* (Princeton, N.J.: Van Nostrand Co., 1958).

college, how intensively and how frequently they operated on him, and how close he felt to the people who advised him. Stivers found that those who were well-motivated for college had a significantly greater set of social pressures which had set college as a goal for them. That is, their parents, teachers, friends, and others tended to encourage them strongly to go to college.

d) Intrinsic pleasure in learning.—This factor has not been so thoroughly studied as have the others, perhaps because it is obvious that a person who enjoys studying will go to college if possible. One part of the River City study did shed some light on this part of the theory, however. It was found that able boys with a good school record had more academic interests and hobbies than able boys who were doing only average or poor work in school.

Methods To Be Used To Increase Personal Incentive

The following conclusions can be drawn looking toward a program to increase the motivation of able lower-income boys to go to college.

1. Through an expanded counseling program in the junior and senior high school, identify the able boys not well-motivated for college and inform them and their parents of the possibility of college, and the advantages that might come from it. Also, inform the teachers about this group of boys who are good college material but not likely to go to college unless influenced by the school.

2. Through the skillful use of honor awards, assembly programs, clubs, and other extracurricular activities, and through collaboration with service clubs and other community organizations, increase the social desirability and the social prestige of going to college.

3. Through the academic program of the school, and through selecting and training teachers, make schoolwork more interesting and more rewarding to these boys. This is the crucial thing, but it is the least tangible of the three that have been mentioned. Some school programs are more interesting and more challenging to able boys and girls than others—that is a clear fact. Some

teachers make their subjects so interesting that they win students and encourage them to continue a life of study.

4. Provide ample scholarship and loan funds easily accessible to students of the lower-income group. The best known and most highly publicized scholarship programs probably do very little to bring youth from lower-income families to college. These scholarships go to a very highly selected group of people, mainly in the upper 1 percent of ability, and mainly of upper-middle-class family background. For example, the occupations of the fathers of the 900 winners of the National Merit Scholarships in 1958 fall into the following categories: upper and upper-middle class, 73 percent; lower-middle class, 20 percent; upper-lower class, 6.4 percent; lower-lower class, 0.3 percent.

Probably the scholarships carrying the least prestige and the least remuneration are more generally available to students from lower-income families. Also, the current government loan program may be especially good for this group.

Personal Incentive for Higher Education among Girls

The preceding analysis has concerned itself mainly with boys, because the motivation of girls for higher education is decidedly different from that of boys.

A drive for achievement in our society can have two different outlets for girls—one through getting married and becoming a successful wife and mother, and the other through having a business or professional career which usually involves a college education, as with boys.

Girls with superior intellectual ability are likely to feel a good deal of conflict at this point, and to be uncertain about their next steps after high school graduation. Thus Stivers' prediction of college-going was not very accurate for girls, while it was accurate for boys. From his interviews with able girls in the tenth grade, he found 25 to be "non-motivated for college"; and only 3 of this group actually entered college. But of the 38 girls whom he pronounced "well-motivated for college," 12, or almost a third, did not enter college. These girls probably felt some desire to go to college, but during their last two years of high school they decided that marriage and a family were more important. Six of these 12 girls were married by the end of the year following their high school graduation.

The girls in Stivers' study were studied again after their high school graduation. As was the case with boys, those who got the best grades in high school were more likely to go to college. Also, the girls who achieved best in high school relative to their intellectual ability tended to go to college. Probably the motivation of the girls who had decided to go to college kept their school grades high, while others of equal ability who were not going to college demanded less of themselves in their schoolwork.

In contrast to the boys, there was not much relation between social class and college-going among the able girls. Probably the desire for marriage and a home is about equally distributed among the various social classes, although a number of upper-middle-class girls see their way clear to marrying the kind of man they want through going to college and perhaps meeting him there.

There was a reliable superiority of the college-going girls over the non-college-going ones on the California Psychological Inventory, as was true in the case of boys.

These findings and similar ones in other studies indicate that conclusions about personal incentive of able girls for college is a different and more complex problem than it is with boys. One should not expect to see large increases in the numbers of able girls going to college and on into professional work under present social conditions.

Encouraging Personal Incentive for Higher Education among Rural Youth

GLYN MORRIS

Assistant Superintendent in Charge of Pupil Personnel,
Lewis County, New York

IN LOOKING AT THE PROBLEM UNDER CONSIDERATION AS IT RELATES to rural youth, nothing seems so relevant in describing the complexity of the over-all situation as the statement "Percents, ratios, and numbers are interesting but not predictive in the individual case."

Let me illustrate what I mean with just a few random examples. The little village of Jefferson in mountainous Schoharie County in central New York State has a population of less than 500 and a central school of about 300 pupils, kindergarten through twelfth grade. While visiting there last June, I was told by the principal that, in 1957, 20 pupils were graduated from high school. The senior class took eight of the twenty state scholarships available to the 250-or-so seniors throughout the county, and 11 graduates went on to a four-year, degree-granting college. In 1958, 10 were graduated from high school, 2 won state scholarships, and 8 went on to four-year, degree-granting colleges. In 1959, 15 were graduated, 2 won state scholarships, and 9 went on to college. This is a good record.

Size of population and other characteristics, including income, median educational level of the population, and percentage of foreign born in Schoharie County, are almost identical with Lewis County, where I live. Approximately 25 percent of Lewis County high school graduates go on to a four-year college. We estimate about 15 percent of those capable of doing college work do not. According to the principal at Jefferson, the factor contributing most to the achievement I have reported is the positive attitude toward education of a segment of the population, namely Germans whose ancestors lived in the Palatinate. In Lewis County, until recently, the group most vocal in opposing education after age sixteen were the Mennonites—also of German extraction.

Now, let us switch to Washington County, Maine, where the median level of educational achievement for the entire population is approximately a year more than for either Lewis or Schoharie County in New York State. Foreign-born population is less than 1 percent (excluding Canadians). Here, I am told, 19.5 percent go on to four-year colleges, and more than 60 percent in the upper half of the senior class do not go on. Eleven of the 19 high schools have fewer than four teachers. The dropout rate from grades 8–12 is given as 56 percent. Washington County, with more than a third again the population of Lewis County, has 110 college graduates in residence; Lewis has 290, and Schoharie 470. But the median income per family for Washington County is $1,800 compared with $2,500 for Lewis and Schoharie.

I was recently told by a school official in West Virginia of a community which is within twenty miles of a college, but from which no high school graduate had gone to any college in the preceding five years.

Finally, among these vignettes, I must include one item on the state of Kentucky, where in 1950 (I presume there's been some change since then) only one out of ten pupils who had started in the first grade twelve years before, even finished high school, and where the median score for 250 ninth-graders on a well-known group intelligence test was 84. This tenuous appraisal, which illustrates the limitations of standardized testing for pupils of limited background, was compounded by the fact that the median nonverbal scores were lower than the verbal.

Indeed, there are degrees of rurality and, occasionally superimposed on this, some interesting exceptions to the over-all pattern of college-going by children of farmers—that is, rural folk—although a relationship between the socioeconomic level of the home and community and aspiration is unmistakable. A common denominator throughout is undoubtedly the poor quality of program embracing both facilities and personnel offered in many rural high schools, which are frequently inferior to urban schools—with exceptions, to be sure. In many quarters the panacea most strongly advocated for this condition is more money and reorganization. However much both of these are needed, the effects of just this solution are somewhat qualified when we recall that adequate facilities and programs alone do not change the picture for other groups, for example, the children of laborers and craftsmen. In fact, with respect to the problem we are considering, I find it difficult to distinguish between rural and urban conditions; perhaps the difference is only in some minor details.

About the problem as it concerns rural youth, I make two observations which are presented cautiously:

1. Inasmuch as the amount of stimulation provided by pupils for each other may be quantitatively small in a rural school, this may have some bearing on aspiration—all else being equal. For instance, by bringing together five talented pupils from five small schools for a weekly seminar on the humanities of a very high level, free-wheeling type involving philosophic problems, we have some evidence that a few of this group have raised their sights. The association was beneficial.

2. My second observation has to do with what I would term psychological isolation, and this concerns me most. In my first-hand, intensive contacts with a limited number of talented but unmotivated youngsters, I detect one characteristic common to them all. They appear to have personal problems of considerable magnitude, the nature of which is hidden from them. I am not unaware that this, too, may be just another detail of the socioeconomic determinant. But let me describe what I mean. Frequently these youngsters are socially isolated. They live on the outskirts of a rural community, sometimes in housing of a low order. Often there is conflict in the home, or problems of a kind we associate with maladjusted children. The home is disorganized. One or both parents are at odds with the world. And when we follow these youngsters after graduation they continue to make unsatisfactory decisions.

Again, I am not unmindful that this condition exists even in communities of very high socioeconomic level, as, for instance, in one community in suburban New York, where the median IQ is 120 and median income $11,000, I was told by the principal that many of his pupils had their own private psychiatrist. Over-indulgence produces the same results as neglect.

But to return to rural youth. It seems to me that, for all the validity of the socioeconomic determinant, the problem has another dimension which may or may not be related to it. These youngsters give evidence of a low self-concept or self-image, and it is to this area we might look, as well as to others, if we are to know more about what impedes their progress toward higher achievements.

If this is true, then this offers a clue as to what is possible in helping them. Obviously, we cannot change a community or a culture. Value systems change only slowly. But under the right circumstances, individuals can transcend their environment. A psychiatrist, working with some of our pupils, once said to me, "We can't change their environment, but we can help youngsters develop insight and ego and strength to cope with it." I think this suggests an important line for investigation.

This means strengthening and broadening guidance programs in the fullest sense of the word. Furthermore, this means early iden-tification of potentially able pupils, and, through case conferences, continuous counseling, and procedures for enhancing the individ-ual, giving him opportunity to gain insight and to develop a sense of his own worth. It has been demonstrated that effective coun-seling does help individuals mature. It should do more than pro-vide educational and occupational information and help pupils make schedules. To get the right answers, we must ask the right questions; so, I suggest that, even as we acknowledge the restric-tions of environment on a youngster's vision and reassert that we must work with parents and social agencies to provide all the cultural enrichment possible, we must also take a good look at the way in which these forces affect the pupil's self-concept and look more deeply over a longer period at the inner life of the pupil, as well as the nature of his particular world. By a more thorough application of what we have long known about what makes peo-ple behave as they do, we may be able to see the world through his eyes—and consequently direct his vision to a program of larger self-realization.

Personal Incentive for Higher Education among Deprived Groups

RICHARD L. PLAUT

President, National Scholarship Service and Fund
for Negro Students

THERE ARE THREE REASONS WHY I THINK IT WILL BE MORE REWARD-
ing to discuss personal incentive in culturally and economically
deprived groups rather than in minority groups, even at the risk
of running into some overlap with Professor Havighurst.

First of all, ethnic minorities usually are predominant among
deprived groups; conversely, there is a high incidence of under-
privilege among ethnic minorities. Second, the same educational
factors are operating among the underprivileged whether they are
Negroes, Puerto Ricans, or Kentucky mountaineers. Third, it will
avoid the trap of defining a minority group. As you know, this
inevitably ends up in the *reductio ad absurdum* that everyone belongs to a minority group except males (or is it now females?)
and your "in-laws."

The one problem which the deprived do not necessarily share
with some minorities is discrimination or segregation, whether
legal, *de facto,* or self-segregation. But these are separate issues
on which we could spend the entire day, profitably no doubt but
nevertheless digressing from the issues which we have been as-
signed. Accordingly, I shall by-pass the educational effects of
segregation with the observation that, quite aside from being
morally wrong, segregation inevitably leads to a downward spiral
of educational regression, damaging, unequally it is true, but
still damaging the segregators as well as the segregated.

Cultural and economic deprivation leads to a significant educational lag between deprived groups and the rest of our population.
The educational lag leads to inequality of educational opportunity, cuts deeply into our supply of trained manpower, and serves
to block our traditional social and economic mobility. Much,

therefore, is at stake, including the growing trend towards "two-class" cities, rich and poor, with the middle classes moving out to the suburbs.

How do we go about helping the victims of the educational lag catch up? Recently, when I saw a superb, moving play *The Miracle Worker*, I found a poignant analogy to our topic. The play is about eight-year-old Helen Keller and the terrifying, fierce struggle to find a way to communicate with this extraordinarily intelligent, blind, deaf, and mute child, then hopelessly rebellious, belligerent, and spoiled. The wonderful breakthrough came when she discovered that the hand games she had been playing with her teacher spelled out words and that words meant not only things and people she could feel and touch, but ideas she could understand. Overwhelmed by newly discovered pleasures of the mind, her tantrums stopped. She was too busy learning. At this moment, she became to me just another deprived child, who hadn't been able to use words she'd never heard and who turned from a household delinquent to a child of unsuspected capabilities who later would be a superb citizen, when the world of ideas and the words with which to communicate opened up to her.

To return to the more usual kinds of deprivation, we must first identify those with good minds and educational potential early enough for them to catch up in the growingly competitive race. Second, we must help those identified to change their own, as well as their parents', images of themselves: the image of themselves as permanent strugglers for survival to one in which going to college is not only possible but likely—not just for the sake of going to college but to prepare for careers for which college training is necessary. Third, we must then teach them sufficient competence in the basic academic skills of communication with both words and numbers so that they may ultimately qualify, not only for admission to college but for the financial aid most of them will need.

In taking a look back at these three "musts," I am reminded of the attempt of a television public relations man, in the early days of television, to answer for an earnest inquirer, the question "Just how does television work?" "Oh, that's simple," was his reply.

"Over here, there is a camera; over there, there is a TV set; and, in between, there is a miracle."

I have had the good fortune and the great satisfaction in the past three years, to have shared in the passing of just such a miracle.

Some of you have heard of the Demonstration Project in New York City's Junior High School No. 43 and George Washington High School, cosponsored by the New York City Board of Education, the College Entrance Examination Board, and the National Scholarship Service and Fund for Negro Students.

The population of J.H.S. No. 43 is approximately 45 percent Negro, 40 percent Puerto Rican, 15 percent "other." The area and its population are poor, very poor. From the last pre-project class of about 200 going on from J.H.S. No. 43 to George Washington High School, exactly 9 had gone on to some form of post-high-school education. The dropout rate had been high; the disciplinary problems, many and tough.

In the first project class, now seniors in George Washington High School, there are about 40 students who are doing creditable work in five major academic subjects, who are reasonably promising college candidates, and, most importantly, who *want* and intend to go to college. (Incidentally this class only started the project in the ninth grade and therefore had a minimum of project benefits.)

The average project student began the project, reading 1.4 years below grade level. In 2.6 years his reading jumped from a level of 5.4 to 9.7. For the first time in the history of J.H.S. No. 43, the project students are reading well above grade level.

The dropout rate has been halved, and disciplinary problems have virtually disappeared.

How was this miracle brought about? We could spend the rest of the day with the answers to this question, but these are the chief ingredients:

First, money. An average of about $90,000 per year has been invested in the project, divided between the two schools. With an earlier start in elementary school, with more schools involved, and invaluable experience applied, the job can be done for much less, but it will always cost money.

Second, people. The money is spent largely for more professionals of high quality. The principal and his guidance and teaching staff were and must be not only of outstanding professional competence but also must have a deep conviction, amounting to dedication, that the goals are attainable. The success of the experiment is mainly due to Principal Daniel Schreiber's imaginative and often inspired leadership.

Third, identification. Here we started with the familiar dilemma. On the one hand, to try to predict academic potential among culturally deprived children with instruments loaded with the culture of which they have been deprived; on the other hand, using instruments devoid of that culture is equally self-defeating. In the absence of a single magic instrument, a ten-factor profile was developed including verbal and nonverbal tests, classroom performance, and teacher judgment. Teacher judgment, going back full circle to the pretesting era, perhaps proved the most useful tool.

Fourth, changing the image. Individual and group guidance, almost to the saturation point; continuous discussion of higher-level careers; cultural exposure in the form of trips to the theater, the opera, music, ballet, museums, college campuses; giving status to outside reading; involving parents, on these socioeconomic levels, to an almost unheard of degree. All these activities, after a while, caused these children to think about college as naturally as any group of middle-class children.

Fifth, the academic skills. Remedial teachers, small classes, enriched programs, and intensive guidance all contributed to the general rise in achievement and aspiration.

Finally, the new superintendent of schools, Dr. John J. Theobald, with characteristic vision and courage, within the first three or four months of his incumbency, and before the experiment had passed the halfway point, made and has since implemented plans to extend these benefits to 44 other schools, involving more than 60,000 children. The new program, called "Higher Horizons," starts at the third grade and involves non-college-bound children as well. Because the program starts at an earlier level, the cost will be only $20,000 per school per year. Dr. Theobald has wisely assigned Dan Schreiber as coordinator of the entire program.

Stimulated by the events in New York, and Community Talent Search, a NSSFNS activity, a number of other large cities have planned or are planning similar programs. Superintendent Hansen has programs going in Washington at McFarland Junior High School and Roosevelt High School, for example. By the next academic year, up to 500,000 children in various parts of the nation may be affected.

All this represents a significant change in the focus and direction of educational opinion since the 1953 NSSFNS Southern Project, described by Frank Bowles as "the first systematic talent search ever carried on in America." During the past month alone, NSSFNS in one way or another has been involved in five different activities, including this conference, under the aegis of five different agencies, each concerned with talent searching or the educational problems of disadvantaged youth. In addition, we know of at least three more activities with which we have not been directly involved. That is a long way in a short time since the pioneering job in this field undertaken by NSSFNS six years ago and carried on step by step through these years.

Personal incentive, among deprived children in general and minority groups in particular, is being significantly pushed across the land. With this push, the educational lag is being reduced. In time, there may be no lag, provided that we keep in mind that it is only the proliferation, in the very recent past, of more minds, more energy, and more money focused on this problem that has brought about events like this conference, last week's CEEB Colloquium, Project 43, and the several other activities now going on. There will be no lasting solutions from one point of view, one attack, one conference, one foundation grant. This is a serious national problem and requires a multiplicity of thinking, experiments, points of view, and approaches—none should be rejected without trial or, at least, a long look by knowledgeable people who really want a resolution.

Discussion Following Panel Statements

Presiding: RALPH F. BERDIE

CHAIRMAN BERDIE: We are now ready for questions or comments.

HORACE MANN BOND (Dean, School of Education, Atlanta University): I would like to ask Dr. Havighurst how one can maintain categories of classes when he makes an historical analysis. Obviously, the lower classes move upward so that in 1960 they are scarcely the same as they were in 1920. Have you any variations in class names to take care of that?

DR. HAVIGHURST: I don't know whether names make much difference. I get your point. Of course, there has been a major shift in the income and values of lower-, middle-, and upper-working-class groups. This is one of the things that has made possible this enormous increase in people going to college. You are right that in 1920 each of these groups had different cultural values and different ideas about college education. There is also some difference in size which I haven't taken account of, as you indicated.

DR. THEOBALD: As several panelists pointed out, our greatest loss of talent is among the deprived children of the lower classes. Except in rare instances, we have done almost nothing to stimulate the homes and parents of these children, and, until we do reach the homes more effectively, I don't think we can really understand the problem or do much about it. Mr. Shulman, who has done a splendid job along these lines, can speak from first-hand experience.

DAVID SHULMAN (Counselor, George Washington High School, New York City): I consider reaching the home one of the most important factors in trying to determine why children don't go on to further their education. We have tried very hard to reach some parents, but only with limited success. At least half the children in our group have lost one or both parents, not so often through death as through desertion. The many problems that confront the family create certain tensions and frustrations. These may lead to rejection or violence on the part of the parent toward the child and antagonism or withdrawal on the part of the latter. The child may become determined to sever the bonds with his family by leaving school, finding a job, and striking out on his own.

We employ the usual methods of communication with the home by phone, personal visits, and letters in English or Spanish. Where the parent is uninterested or ineffectual, I try to reach an older brother or sister, grandparent, or aunt, or other relative who has a positive relationship with the child. Sometimes there are neighbors or friends who have won the respect and affection of the child. Sometimes the family relationships change. A boy who has lived with his mother for a year or two may be sent to live with his father or another relative.

I have been able to interest some adults in playing the role of big brother or sister to some of these children. A professor at Teachers College, Columbia, learned about the project and asked whether he might help in any way. I suggested that he become the mentor of a boy whose mentally ill father had completely withdrawn from family affairs. He consented to do so after I had briefed him on the boy's background, personality, and needs. The boy has been seeing this professor regularly. The professor has taken him on a tour of different branches of the college, has discussed various problems and future plans, and tutors him in several academic subjects. He also helped the boy to find a part-time job in the college library. The boy's response to this relationship has been a better personal adjustment at home and improved school achievement. He is now determined to go to college.

A lady who is active in civic affairs has taken a like interest in one of our girls. The girl, who comes from a depressed home background filled with conflict and tensions, was ready to drop out of school. This lady has provided not only for the girl's material needs but also her emotional ones. She has given the girl kindness and understanding, encouragement and friendship. The girl spends three days a week in the lady's home, enjoys nourishing food, a quiet place to reflect and study, meets cultured people, and is exposed to stimulating conversation. This relationship has done wonders for the girl. She has remained in school, gained confidence, self-respect, and inner strength to pursue her goal of nursing.

We need more enlightened persons in the community who are willing to give of their time and themselves to show an interest in and guide and encourage young people who come from disadvantaged homes. And we need some who will work with parents, draw them into social and community organizations, motivate them to improve culturally, and help them to acquire a better understanding of, and relationship with, their children. The cultural growth of the parents is bound to accelerate that of their children.

MISS TANNEYHILL: This is a problem that has interested the Urban League also. In the past year we have developed what we call "Tomorrow's Scientists and Technicians," a program along similar lines. This is a community-centered program through which we are trying to get adults in the community interested in young people. In a number of cities we have organized career clubs for boys and girls, and we have recruited men and women, Negro as well as white, from the community to set up the same sort of big-brother and big-sister relationship with the youngsters. These men and women are doing many interesting things to help the boys and girls.

This program verifies what Dr. Havighurst said about incentives depending upon the kind of relationship youth can establish with people who are college people or who hold college in high regard. We have some very encouraging things beginning to develop in communities both in the North and South.

In Columbus, Ohio, a program has been developed with two of the junior high schools. Career club meetings are held in the school building after school hours. The men and women in the community are working directly with the boys and girls. This extends what is done in the school guidance program into the community. We have done a similar job with three junior high schools and six senior high schools in Miami, Florida, where adults take the boys and girls on trips.   For example, the Miami Urban League arranged a trip to Cape Canaveral for 60 boys and girls and 25 adults, so that they could see what was happening in terms of job development in scientific and technical fields for trained Negroes.   These boys and girls had never had this kind of opportunity before.

The Urban League believes that in the Negro community itself there are a great many resources that have not yet been developed. We are trying to help the fraternal organizations, the fraternities, sororities, and the professional men and women to work more closely with boys and girls to give them the kinds of incentives we feel are greatly needed. Some of the youngsters come from broken homes where there is one parent; others come from families who are interested in having their children go on for higher education but who can do little themselves to give them motivation.

Mrs. Nellie Rosebaugh (Director of College Guidance, Glenville High School, Cleveland, Ohio): When we learn the interests of a student in our school, we assign that student to a certain teacher for an interview.   In this way we involve him through our faculty in our guidance program.

I think of the art teacher.   We send him those students who might be interested in commercial art and architecture.   We expect him to be well informed and to be able to give his students information which they cannot get from home.   Our nurse is most helpful.   She takes the students interested in nursing as early as the tenth grade.   We do this in all fields, and we get our teachers interested in the entire program, which, I think, is very necessary.

Then we invite our college students back each December.   We select certain groups to go to the English classes, the science classes, and the mathematics classes, where they relate their experiences to the tenth-, eleventh-, and twelfth-graders.   To have someone who actually has entered college talk to these students has been most helpful and inspiring.   My school, by the way, is 99 percent Negro.

Mr. Plaut: I would like to say a word about Mrs. Nellie Rosebaugh, because I think anything she says should be listened to pretty carefully. In this 99 percent Negro school that she describes, in the eleven years this activity has been going on, she has helped to produce more highly qualified college candidates for the National Scholarship Service and Fund for Negro Students every year than any other high school in the United States. I am certain this is not coincidental or accidental.

Herbert L. Wright (Youth Secretary, National Association for the Advancement of Colored People): I would like to relate a little story that illustrates something important. A couple of years ago, I was in a certain school visiting a teacher who taught the fourth grade. She said, "Mr. Wright, I want you to meet Fred." She put her arms around Fred's shoulders and said, "You know, Fred is going to make a fine college student some day."

Naturally, that comment interested me. I talked to Fred a little about college and his plans; then, later I went back to see his teacher. Knowing she is a pretty discerning and clever person, I asked, "Was there any particular reason why you said this about Fred?"

She said, "Yes, a very real reason. None of Fred's people has ever gone to college. His father and mother did not even go to high school. Since he is very bright, I just keep reminding him in whatever way I can that he ought to go to college some day."

I thought this was a very grand thing, and I told her so. If we ever make any studies of what this kind of influence can do, I think the results will amaze us.

Dr. Theobald: This is precisely the kind of encouragement that Project 43 seeks to provide.

Dr. Herbert Wright: I understand that. I believe that this teacher was doing a grand job for the little boy. But that is just my opinion. I have no evidence that this simple thing makes a great difference; however, I am confident that it does. Have we had any studies of this that you know of, Dr. Havighurst?

Dr. Havighurst: There have been a few recent studies of the factors that increase motivation for college, investigations of what family, neighborhood, and school influences have played on the youngster. These studies depend pretty largely on the student's own report, and they usually show just what you have suggested, namely, that at the elementary school level and at the secondary school level, those well motivated for college were more likely to have had this kind of influence you describe. There is no question about the efficacy of this kind of personal influence, although there is some question about its relative efficacy at different age levels. I would bet a great deal that one dollar spent in the first grade is worth five dollars spent in the eighth grade as far as incentive for higher education is concerned.

CHAIRMAN BERDIE: Edward Scannon identified a large number of talented high school graduates in 1927. He followed them up twenty years later and compared the ones who went to college with those who did not. Most of those who did not go to college reported that nobody in their own school careers had ever talked with them about going to college; they remembered no discussion at any time as to the possibilities or the advisability of going to college.

WARREN G. FINDLEY (Assistant Superintendent for Pupil Personnel Services, Board of Education of the City of Atlanta, Georgia): I would like to ask a question, but I want to preface it with the statement that I am honestly seeking information and that I am not trying to cast doubts on this plan of enlisting adults to encourage youngsters who receive no encouragement at home.

In setting up this kind of program, how can the old charity approach be avoided? Even if the children don't feel any condescension, won't the parents sometimes resent other adults coming in to "rescue" their children from the mire of their family circumstances and to "elevate" them to a higher plane. I dislike using these terms but I am trying to ask the question so that it can be answered clearly.

MISS TANNEYHILL: We have not found any resistance on the part of the parents. They have sometimes been indifferent, but they have not been hostile. In many instances, parents have been very eager to cooperate. In one or two instances we found that we had to do a lot of groundwork with the youngsters who resisted the adult attention they were beginning to get. The program had to be explained to them and worked out slowly, but it did not result in a feeling of condescension.

Mr. Plaut: One of the experiments we tried (and I think Dan Schreiber will agree that it was highly successful) was to send some of our recent alumni to meetings of parents and children. These were young people with whom the students and the parents could identify themselves both racially and socioeconomically. They were living examples of "I-made-it-so-can-you," and they did not give the impression of looking down at all.

Dr. Theobald: There is a counseling job to be done with the parents as well as with the children. We must approach this problem from the counseling standpoint, and use all the maturity and skill that the trained counselor has. One of the most striking demonstrations of successful parental counseling comes from Project 43, where the ratio of parents freely seeking interviews shifted from 1 to 10 to 10 to 1. The school created an atmosphere in which the people with the skills were sought out for help and advice. I wonder if Dan Schreiber will say something about that. He has done a remarkable job in enlisting the cooperation of parents.

Mr. Schreiber: My feeling is that the schools must start working with parents very early in the child's development in order to foster positive attitudes toward education. The school should start counseling the parents during kindergarten, not every day but at least once a month, especially during the term preceding admission to school. When the mothers and children report to school, groups of seven to ten children can meet with a librarian or a volunteer who can tell them a story or read to them, while the parents meet with a counselor to discuss topics they indicate a need for.

Children from disadvantaged groups come to school with emotional handicaps. Some of them have never been to birthday parties or family reunions where grandparents coddle them and where relatives exchange gifts. They have never had the feeling of belonging to a well-knit group and of participating in the group's activities.

Some of you may recall the pleasure your child experienced when you first read to him. It may have been a story before bedtime or a story while waiting for dinner. As it became a regular occurrence, you probably asked him to turn the pages for you or to point to a word or to a picture. He learned that one reads from left to right, from top to bottom, and that one turns pages from right to left. When he got to school, he had an advantage. He was complimented by the teacher, because he could read a word or two or could interpret a picture. His initial experiences were broader and deeper than those of the child from the disadvantaged home.

I would like to tell you a story that was told to me at the CEEB Colloquium. The incident happened to a member of the staff while he was riding in a taxi from the subway to the CEEB office. He struck up a conversation with the cab driver and asked him how many days a week he worked. "I work six days," the cab driver replied. "What do you do on your day off?" the staff member asked. "Well," said the cab driver, "I used to see the Giants play or watch the games on TV, but they are no longer in Manhattan. Last week my son said, 'Let's go down to the Museum of Modern Art.' I had never been there, and my wife had never been there, but the boy wanted to; so we went along. I enjoyed it, and I'm going back again." This is the type of improvement we must seek. We must get parents to participate in worthwhile activities; we must involve them, together with their children, in experiences that raise their sights.

David Shulman was the counselor for our first group in which the ratio of parent-initiated to counselor-initiated conferences was 1 to 10. That ratio changed from 1 to 10 to 10 to 1. The parents are now accepting us. We are an integral part of their lives now; we are friends whom they can come to for advice and help. Among his group, Dave has students who tell him the most intimate secrets of the family. I would like to recount one story to show how helpful a counselor can be in keeping a child in school and working toward a worthwhile goal. Dave Shulman was the counselor, and he is too modest to tell you this, but I'm not.

The school noticed that a girl in the senior class had become a truant. Dave checked with the other students and discovered that the girl had run away from home because the situation there had become unbearable. Dave sent word to the girl to come in to see him. She told him why she had left her home. After a lengthy conference, which was attended by the social worker, the girl agreed that she would return to school; however, she would not tell where she was staying for fear that her mother would force her to return home. The school accepted this. On the very same day, Dave and the social worker went to see the mother at her place of work. They spent more than an hour there discussing the family situation. The girl is back in school regularly now and living under supervision outside the home with the mother's approval. This is the kind of guidance we must provide if we are going to resolve the problems of disadvantaged youngsters.

CHAIRMAN BERDIE: We have spent a considerable amount of time discussing the very interesting and stimulating New York project this afternoon. I wonder if it would not be a good idea now to turn to some of the other programs and projects that are under way and to bring up other questions or topics that you would like to discuss.

FREDERICK H. JACKSON (Executive Associate, Carnegie Corporation of New York, New York City): There is a very modest man sitting on the other side of the hall who has a project that he ought to tell you about.

CLYDE VROMAN (Director of Admissions, University of Michigan): I sense that in this group we are, like the Egyptian mummy, "pressed for time," and that there isn't time for any modest people! As you know, that was Frederick Jackson, a representative of the Carnegie Corporation, speaking. When he says, "Won't you tell them about one of our projects," who am I to remain modest? Seriously, to tell you about this project I really should have about fifteen minutes to be assured you go away with a proper understanding.

You asked for projects that are going on. As I listened to the discussion last night and today, I got the feeling that your real concern is "What can we do about it?" We agree on the problem. We have heard the definitions of the problems many times. I am convinced the need now is to get to the people who are working with the children all the time and to get such people doing more of the right things for such children. I think that the reason Dan Schreiber and these other people are getting things done is that they are right there working with the children. I think that is the most important point of this whole conference. We undoubtedly need more research on some aspects of this problem. But most of the research that has been done in the last decade has run in cycles and now rests on the shelf. It leaves us with the gnawing problem: What are we going to do about it?

In the North Central Association of Colleges and Secondary Schools, in which I am an officer and have worked for years, we started to study the problem of articulation of high schools and colleges. Among other areas of concern, we studied the special problems of talented students. We are, of course, also interested in helping all students, including the group in the lower quarter.

One of the results of this committee work was a request to the Carnegie Corporation of New York for a grant to support a project entitled "The Identification, Guidance, and Motivation of Superior and Talented Students." We believe that one must first identify these students and then, as an initial step in motivating them, give them the hope that they can go to college, the conviction that it is worthwhile to go to college, and the confidence that they can start doing something about it.

From 3,400 NCA schools, we selected 100 that met certain criteria, one of which was that they not have more than 30 to 35 percent of their students going to college and another was that they have a substantial proportion of their top-quarter students *not* going to college. We now are in the second year of our project and have involved these schools in action programs within their communities. We invited the principal or assistant principal and the counselor from each of the 100 high schools to one of five five-day workshops in the summer of 1958. Thus, during that summer of 1958, we had 200 people come from 100 high schools for a five-day training period. Using all the resources we could provide them in this series of five workshops, these 200 school people cooperatively planned the first-year projects in their schools.

We now are in the second year of the program and have identified more than 20,000 top-quarter students. We have Stouffer's "Your Educational Plan" inventory as well as much other information on each student, in the central office in Chicago. We have two full-time directors.

Last summer (1959) we had a second series of five five-day workshops for the same persons from the 100 schools in the project. We believe that these persons in the NCA schools can do a great deal to help talented students and increase the proportion of youngsters going to college. Through identification, guidance, motivation, and preparation, these 100 schools are doing some amazing things.

In Marshall, Michigan, a little town of four or five thousand, the proportion of seniors going to college was very small. The school identified about 125 talented students. I remember vividly the first meeting at Marshall High School in the fall of 1958, when they invited me and one of the project directors to address the parents. They sent out personal letters of invitation to the parents of the identified talented students. They expected about 50 to 75 parents to show up, and they intended to meet in a small gymnasium in the elementary school. When the meeting began, although there were only 125 students in the identified group, 250 parents and relatives of these students were present at the meeting!

We firmly believe that these schools are capable of doing a lot now that they did not know how to do by themselves. The assurance of knowing that there was an organized program they could join seemed to make a difference. Although about half of the schools were already trying to do something, the NCA served as a catalyst in helping them move forward. The two most important problems encountered by the project schools, after identifying these students, were (1) how to teach these superior students and how to give them a better preparation for college, and (2) how to get teachers to do a more thorough and stimulating job of teaching.

This is one project now going on quietly. We do not want to give it extensive publicity until we can evaluate it more completely. It is going very well. We think we have something very worthwhile in terms of involving people, getting things done, and finding out from the schools the help that they need from the outside. Further information can be procured by writing to Dr. J. Ned Bryan, NCA Superior and Talented Student Project, 57 West Grand Avenue, Chicago 10, Illinois.

Dr. Daughtry: I wonder if colleges and universities are actually carrying their part of this burden. There is a feeling among some institutions that this business of recruiting is unethical unless the student happens to be a halfback or tackle! I just wonder what the results would be if we really gave wholehearted assistance to high school guidance people and administrators. In our state, I know of high schools in which there are superior students who have never been visited by any college or university representative. I think that we know a great many things that we can do along these lines, but we are just not doing them.

Mr. Monro: I am glad Dr. Daughtry raised this point, because it brings to mind a notion that I have had for some time and that was refreshed by Dr. Darley's talk. The notion is that the colleges are still competing rather stupidly for students. It occurs to me that the colleges might accomplish a lot if they were somehow able to pool their efforts for recruiting students, especially in poor high schools where it doesn't pay any one of them to make a regular annual visit but where it might be worthwhile for a number of colleges, acting together, to send a man in.

Everyone knows the typical pattern. In a good suburban high school there are often two or three hundred talented, well-certified seniors bound for college. Scores of admissions officers will go to such a school each year; yet, in the context of what we are saying here, these efforts are virtually wasted since all of these students would go to college anyway. In suburban Chicago every good high school has two or three hundred college visitors a year, whereas in downtown Chicago the schools have hardly any—unless there is a football player in the school.

Whatever shape a cooperative organization takes, it clearly ought to represent all kinds of colleges, large and small, public and private. The effort ought to be double-edged. The first purpose should be to get the idea across everywhere that the colleges are eager to help able students, no matter what their school or background. And the second purpose should be to develop in the colleges themselves a sense of their real responsibilities to work effectively on this problem. I think it is terribly important to develop the idea that this effort is a joint responsibility of our colleges, acting as a community.

The colleges that joined in this kind of enterprise would naturally have to put money and time into it, perhaps an amount per capita in their freshman classes. All of them could share in enlisting and supporting a staff whose object would be to visit and encourage talented students all over the place, to work up lists of able students everywhere, and to keep tabs on them. Such an effort would not need to be expensive, but it could be awfully powerful.

A. F. TUTTLE (Director of Admissions, Stetson University): In Florida, after hemming and hawing and backing and filling, we have finally established a state-wide "College Day" program in which college representatives from the middle of September to the middle of February visit practically every school in our state. This means that from twelve to eighty representatives from different colleges go to each school. This program is worked out jointly by the principals, deans, counselors, registrars, and admissions officers. It is arranged so that the representatives will visit no more than one school a day and have a chance to spend some time talking with the counselors and principals. In addition, the colleges try to bring to their campuses each year the high school guidance counselors.

CHAIRMAN BERDIE: May I pose one question? The programs that I know affect mainly those students who have incentive. It is a matter only of directing them to one college or another. Now, how does this affect the students who lack incentive?

MR. TUTTLE: In many of the poorer schools, the limitations of the physical plant preclude a regular schedule on College Day; therefore, by force of circumstances, most juniors and seniors, whether they want to or not, are exposed at least to three different college representatives. Of course, the effectiveness of the exposure depends again on whether the school is able to do anything prior to and after the exposure.

DR. THEOBALD: Mr. Chairman, may I stick my neck way out on this? To begin with, the average college today is in competition with others to get the best of the pupils who have already decided to go to college. If we really want to encourage youngsters who have ability to go on to higher education regardless of resources and previous interest, we have to go after them in almost the same way that some colleges go after athletes. Faculty members and alumni have to keep an eye out for the student who has potential; they have to stimulate and encourage him while he is in high school. The percentage of able youngsters going to college will not increase if we merely deal with those who already hold college as their objective.

I was president of a liberal arts college. I don't think it was any different from the others in many ways. We looked down our noses at our teacher education department, and we even debated occasionally whether or not the members of this department had a right to talk on the floor of the faculty assembly. I suspect this was par for the course. When you have such a barrier between the college and the high school, it is no wonder that little is accomplished in the way of cooperation.

In general, there is a real barrier between the colleges and the very people they have trained in their "outcast" departments of education, and I think one of the most important things colleges could do is to pay an awful lot more attention to building a common interest between the high school and the college teachers. After all, the colleges educate the teachers who, in turn, educate their prospective students. How can they afford to be indifferent?

DR. MONRO: Most colleges have terribly busy admissions officers; they put incredible amounts of energy into their field work. If just a small amount of this energy were diverted into the general problem, this would help tremendously.

Furthermore, colleges use alumni to recruit in communities where their own admissions officers can't go for lack of time and money. Sure, many of them start out by being interested in the football team, but it isn't long before they are interested in the other students whom they are meeting. Hundreds of colleges across the country must have four or five alumni who are ready to graduate to a higher stage of search in their own community. It strikes me that somehow or other we need to persuade the college community that we have both an interest and a responsibility to work together on this thing and not to regard this as a competitive area.

CHAIRMAN BERDIE: Shall we have some reactions from some of the people in high schools?

MRS. ROSEBAUGH: When Joe Jefferson came to our school this year, he said, "I won't talk just about my college. Just bring together some boys you think ought to go to college, and I will talk about college." He did a splendid job.

FRANK H. BOWLES (President, College Entrance Examination Board): When we get all dressed up, we must be certain we have some place to go.

Mr. Brierly and I collaborated last spring in a state meeting which was devoted partly to the encouragement of talent. I remember talking there with the principal of a high school in a community with the impossible name of "Swink." The principal of Swink High School said that he had two above-average girls who were graduating in June and that he had listened with interest to what we had to say about scholarships and loans. Although they were the best students he had ever had in the Swink High School, these girls were only "B" students. He thought they might have been "A" students if there had been any other students in that high school of this caliber to challenge them. What were these girls going to do? They did not have good enough averages to get a scholarship in any college in that state. They did not have sufficient family support to be willing to risk a loan. They did not know what their occupation would be, even if they did go to college. It was all very well to talk.

I would be very much in favor of having the colleges pool their resources for recruitment, and we have discussed this in some CEEB meetings. One of the problems, however, is that the colleges with sufficient resources to lend support to this enterprise are not likely to be willing to abide by its broad objectives. They are not particularly interested in the "second-class" students of whom there might be a fair number.

Wholesale encouragement is likely to backfire, I fear. Suppose you go to a high school with twenty-five or fifty seniors and build up interest. Suppose you stimulate real enthusiasm for college and turn up only "B" students. What then are you going to do? How long can you keep a high school really participating? How long can you keep a student body really interested unless somebody is willing to take their best students, that is, the "B" students? Remember that there are a great many more "B" students than there are "A" students.

By all means, let's do personal missionary work in schools, but, if we do, let us be certain that we are willing to take the consequences of what we turn up and that we do not dampen the enthusiasm we arouse by saying, "What you have done just isn't good enough."

Climate of Opinion

JOHN M. STALNAKER

President, National Merit Scholarship Corporation

MANY YEARS AGO, AN ABLE YOUNG FRESHMAN AT HARVARD ASKED Professor Alfred North Whitehead what courses he was teaching that semester. Professor Whitehead replied that he was giving Whitehead I, Whitehead II, and Whitehead III. Following the example of this distinguished professor, I generally speak on National Merit Scholarship I and National Merit Scholarship II and then offer a seminar on what NMSC research is revealing. Today, however, my remarks concern the Merit program and its influence on the climate of opinion. In a larger sense, these comments are pertinent to the purpose of this conference.

The National Merit Scholarship program is a fascinating project charged with human interest, aimed at serious and important objectives, and dedicated to the welfare of the nation. It is an ongoing, action program. We use what we believe are the best instruments and procedures; we do not await the development of perfection. Where necessary, we devise the best things we can. The show must go on, and it does, for every year we select additional winners. We subject our operation to constant study, and we earnestly seek advice and help from every competent source. Every year, in our opinion, we improve.

The purpose of the Merit program is to see, to the extent that it is able, that no high school senior of unusual academic promise is prevented for financial reasons from attending the college of his choice. There are secondary purposes which may be even more important. The Merit program makes available, without charge or fee, a common mechanism for corporations and other donors to use in offering their own sponsored scholarships. At present, we have about one hundred such sponsors.

The chief impact of the program, however, has been to help create a climate of opinion in which intellectual competence may be honored and may thrive. We think we are succeeding when we hear, as we did recently from a roving admissions officer of an Eastern college, that the Merit program has created an atmosphere in which a scholar is a more acceptable person to the general public. We strive to elevate the place of intellectual training in the eyes of teachers, students, and the public, and to make the public more aware of what the schools are doing in the training of the mind.

These objectives are accomplished to the extent that they are by a national scholarship competition. It is an intellectual contest with a certain amount of fanfare and publicity. Here, for once, is a dramatic event in which the public has its eyes focused on the intellectual side of schoolwork. Here is an instance where schools are talked about but no mention is made of football or basketball. We do not honor the glee clubs or the marching bands. We do not call public attention to student misbehavior, to the automobile problem, or to the problems of going steady, but to the real purpose of the school, namely, training the mind. And the public has shown a lively interest in this activity.

The National Merit Scholarship Corporation is a private, independent, not-for-profit, Illinois corporation, established in the summer of 1955, with funds totaling $20 million granted by the Ford Foundation and $500,000 granted by the Carnegie Corporation. The program has been scheduled for a trial period of ten annual selections. Four of these have been completed, and the students are now in college. The fifth is in progress, and the winners will be announced in May. Five more programs are scheduled to be held, one each year.

Other donors have joined in our efforts and have added another $6 million. We hope, as time goes on, to raise a good deal more money. The Merit Corporation is controlled by a distinguished board of directors, including educators and business leaders, with Laird Bell the chairman. He has been chairman of the board of trustees of the University of Chicago, chairman of the board of trustees of Carleton College, chairman of the board of the Weyerhaeuser Timber Company, and on the board of overseers of Harvard.

The National Merit Scholarship Corporation does not sell tests or profit from the sale of tests. Our services for sponsors in the Merit program are given without overhead or any fee or retainer charge of any kind. Every cent contributed by a sponsor goes in its entirety to the students and to the colleges.

We publish full reports of our activities. We have no secrets. The method of operation is simple in outline, but complicated in detail. Each year, toward the end of the school year, we invite the schools to offer their juniors a test of educational development. Last year about 550,000 pupils from 14,500 schools participated. The student fee payable to the testing service is $1.00. If any able student cannot afford the fee, we will pay it, so that no able student recommended by his school will be prevented from being in the program.

The test is so designed that we believe the mere taking of it is a valuable educational experience. It consists of exercises of the very type which will be required in college work. The scores are reported to the schools and, through them, to the students. Both a general and a technical manual of interpretation are provided. Local and national norms are given.

Early in the planning it was necessary to decide whether the selection should be made on a national basis or separately for each state, and this is a tender point. What method is the fairest? What method will do the most to encourage and stimulate promising students, students from a deprived background, from every state? Education historically has been state-controlled. It differs from state to state in quality and sometimes in other major ways.

It was decided that, since only 10,000 semifinalists were to be selected, which is less than 1 percent of the senior class, it would be wisest to use a state quota system. This system, in a sense, is a handicapping method which adjusts to some extent the differences in the educational systems of the states. It assumes (and we think with some justification) that if the student in one state had been educated in another state, he would probably have scored differently on the test. Since there are many able students in every state of the Union, it is fairly safe to assume that those in a fraction of the top 1 percent of each state are roughly equal in potential. In any case, from the very start, we have clearly stated that this is the method being followed. The differences in the cutting scores among the states is not great, but in certain places, for example, the District of Columbia, there has been strong objection to the use of state quotas. Washington, D.C., is a special case, since it is a city without rural areas and is not comparable to other states.

Semifinalists are selected exclusively on the basis of test scores. The best in each state are sifted for the top 0.8 of 1 percent of the annual high school graduates of that state. These students are then given a second test, the Scholastic Aptitude Test of the College Board. At the same time, personal data, as well as financial information about the family of the student, are obtained. The names of all semifinalists are printed in a booklet which is widely distributed to colleges and other scholarship-granting agencies.

If the second test confirms the earlier test (and it does in some 99 percent of the cases), the individual becomes a finalist and is technically eligible for a Merit scholarship, and each such student is presented with a Certificate of Merit attesting to his high performance. Were funds available, these students would all be given Merit scholarships. Since the funds are limited, further selection must be made, and a committee of experts goes to work to select among these very superior students.

A sponsor may set up specifications of his own and himself select among these finalists if he wishes. Most of the sponsors do not so desire.

One purpose of the program is to help as many of these finalists as we can, for we consider them all qualified for scholarship support. A Merit scholarship is an award without reference to need. After it is granted, the need is computed along the general lines used by most colleges. Stipends vary from $100 minimum to a $1,500 annual maximum. In some cases of sponsored scholarships, the sponsors may elect to offer a minimum of $250. A grant to the college usually accompanies the scholarship.

In addition to these top awards, some 27,500 other students this year are sent letters of commendation. These students are selected on a national basis. All students with selection scores of 134 or over in the United States will receive a letter of commendation from us signed by the principal as well as by us. The individuals honored by direct recognition will total this year approximately 37,500, or slightly over 2 percent of the high school seniors of the United States, or less than 7 percent of the students tested.

To date, some 3,000 Merit scholars have been named and are in college. They are in about 390 colleges, and they are in all four years—freshman, sophomore, junior, and senior. Because the winner selects his own college and his own course of study and because he is chosen without reference to his college choice, his financial need, or the suitability of his background preparation to the course of studies he has selected, one might expect a number of failures which, of course, we do have.

In our first year of operation, we selected 555 Merit scholars. These students are now seniors in college, but 23 have graduated early, and what a wonderful group these have been! Most graduated with honors, and almost all are going on to further education. In general, the academic records of the entire 555 are superb. They are active individuals who have done excellent work, in general, leading their classes in college in many cases.

Thirty-six of the original group, some 7 percent, have dropped out for one reason or another. We know that 15 dropped out with good academic records at the time they left college, and 21, or about 4 percent, are what we classify as academic casualties. Many of these, however, will re-enter college at some subsequent time. About 10 percent of the original group changed their college without loss of credit or scholarships.

In our second year we had 827 who entered college. They are now juniors, but three of them have graduated already. Of the 26 early graduates (that is, 23 of the first group and 3 of the second group) 21 are entering graduate or professional schools immediately. And as a side comment, I might say that the occupations of the fathers of these 26 early graduates include a farmer whose child is one of six, a telephone line splicer, a motor bus mechanic, a company cashier, a paper hanger, an insurance agent, a superintendent of schools, three college professors, and one college president. The records of our 827 students in this second class thus far have been extremely good, but about 7 percent are dropping out, half of them with deficient scholastic records. Every dropout is a case worthy of study. None should, in our opinion, drop out for academic reasons. Studies of why these few students are failing do not reveal any common pattern. How many failures should one expect in a program of this kind? Can it be reduced much below 4 percent unless the selection is tied much more closely to course of study and to college selection and unless socioeconomic status is given full consideration?

What is the Merit program revealing? What are the main outcomes, the problems? Let us ignore conditions for which we are blamed and over which we have no control. Let us consider a few points of general interest.

In the main, the boys and girls we select are college-bound. They are intellectually very able, and they have high scholastic attainments. They are going to college. While many of them need some financial help, not all do. Of the 10,000 finalists, probably 98 percent will go immediately to college. We call attention to this group of 10,000 and, according to our most recent studies, over 50 percent of them are receiving some kind of scholarship help outside of the Merit program. The "talent loss" among the top 2 percent on our test is not great. These are the students whom everyone seeks. Of our winners, many would go to a different college without the Merit scholarship program.

I urge you not to jump to the conclusion that few of the top 10 or 20 or 30 percent of students need financial help or that all of these students will go to college without financial help. There are many problem cases needing help within these larger groups. It is only when you go to the very top fraction of 1 percent that you find the students with definite plans and a strong determination to go to college.

The Merit money is new money and does not drive out existing scholarship funds. To the extent that it adds to the scholarship pool, it helps one way or another some student who would not otherwise be helped.

Merit scholars, in general, come from above-average economic background. A man high in government office pointed out to me that among the Merit scholars are fewer sons of ditchdiggers and laborers than sons of the professional classes. This observation is correct. The same observation may be made of the President's Cabinet, of which this man was a member. When selection is made without reference to need and at the high school senior level, by what logic would you expect to turn up a preponderance of children of the lowest socioeconomic classes? Why should anybody be surprised by what we are finding when selections are based on developed scholastic ability of the very highest level and are made in the last year of high school?

The influences of superior heredity, superior home environment, superior schools, and superior intellectual climate have measurable effects. Physicians and lawyers and business executives, be they white or colored, are, in the main, able and ambitious people. Their children will, to a reasonable extent, reflect these qualities. To hear some critics, one would think that heredity, home, school, and acculturation are of no importance. Nothing could be further from the truth. Do not underestimate the importance of good schooling and good home environment that has purpose and direction.

Unquestionably, if any segment of the population is forced to live under substandard conditions and deprived of adequate schooling and the right to compete on a fair basis, their educational development will be limited. If you do not measure this development until the end of high school, you will find that the deprivation of these people has had its influence. We must correct the unfair conditions, but we have to do so early in the school years, well before the end of high school.

There is social mobility in this country, however, and we must keep the lanes open and the traffic flowing. Of our 1958 Merit scholars, 77 had fathers who were business executives; 66 had fathers who were engineers; 40, who were physicians; and 55, who were schoolteachers or college teachers. These are the top professions. But let me point out that other Merit scholars had fathers whose occupations were the following: two fathers were barbers; one, a cabinetmaker; one, a cargo checker; six fathers were carpenters; three were cashiers; twenty-five were clerks; one was a college athletic director. There were also a construction worker, a dental technician, three dispatchers, seven electricians, two firemen, a forester, a greenkeeper, a hair stylist, two common laborers, two launderers, eight machinists, three mail carriers, four maintenance men, seven mechanics, two miners, a molder, a mortician, a night kennel man, a male nurse, three painters, a pipe fitter, eight postal clerks, a printer, a proofreader, five repairmen, and so on, down to six who were unemployed. The Merit winners are not limited to those who have three or more bathrooms in their homes.

Let me jump to another area where interest is heavy. The press and the public have used the Merit program to compare schools. This is unfair and unwise. The test results indicate both inherited capacity and the effectiveness of the home and the school. The beauty of the bloom depends upon the quality of the seed, the climate, and the chemicals added to the soil. It is difficult to assess the contributions of each factor independently. Schools differ in size and in purpose and in the quality of the students who attend them. At a recent conference just the last few days here, Paul Woodring is quoted as having said, "A high school diploma from one high school may give evidence of high scholastic attainment, while from another high school in the same city, it may indicate only that the student has been present for four years," and he goes on to say, "We have some of the best schools in the world and some of the worst." Since schools differ, the public is eager for some indication of quality and grasps at the Merit results to give it this indication and, thus, uses the program quite unfairly and unwisely.

In changing the climate of opinion by attracting public interest to intellectual training, the Merit program has a public responsibility. We must direct attention to the main purpose of the schools, but we will need to be patient in correcting misuses of data. Some school officials are worried and harried by this school comparison business, and they point out in defense that the awards in the Merit program are very small relative to participation, and that the program, therefore, does not deserve the public attention it receives. Unless participation in the program is of some value to the schools, it cannot be justified, certainly not on the basis of the probability of any one individual winning a scholarship. However, there are many values besides cash awards. If the program were operated with no cash prizes or scholarships, but only with honors being awarded, the program should still have considerable value.

Merit scholars select their own colleges. We ask them to do so by January 1, because we think they should make up their minds early and give attention to choice of college much earlier than many are now doing. It is also necessary for the sheer mechanics of the program that this be done. We observe the reaction of the student to college and to the wide variation among our colleges. Merit scholars have certain types of preferences. In the market place of bright students, the colleges are rated, and the record of the football team is not the dominant factor. We in the National Merit Scholarship office do not offer guidance or suggest where students should go to college, even when they ask us. We do not believe in mail-order counseling or guidance.

In this conference, we have assumed that college attendance is the proper goal of all talented students, and we apparently have assumed that every able youngster going to any college will benefit from the experience. The problem may be more complex. What is needed is to get the able youth into the kind of college which will stimulate him to develop intellectually. This problem is also highly complicated. Our attention has been focused too much on talent identification and too little on its development.

Colleges differ tremendously in the quality of students they admit. I daresay that the freshmen admitted to some colleges are superior in knowledge and in intellectual skills to the graduates of other colleges. Some accredited colleges have a quarter or more of their entering class unable to read at the eighth-grade level. Colleges differ not only in the quality of the students who enter, but also in the climate that they maintain for learning. In some colleges, athletics, fraternities, and social activities are dominant. At other colleges, sound intellectual development is the main course, not a side dish to be tasted or left untouched.

Colleges also differ socially, but I shall leave this topic, for it is one of the most dangerous ones to talk about.

Still another area of interest has been that of selection. In this conference the assumption has frequently been made that tests are almost infallible instruments, not to be questioned. Aptitude and IQ have become deeply embedded concepts in our thinking; hence, we tend to assume that they are adequate measures of talent. By stressing aptitude to the extent that we have, we have fostered unproductive attitudes in our pupils and in our teachers. Many of the most able youngsters today seem to feel that because they have high native ability for which they have no responsibility, they need not apply themselves to an education. If we allow them to put themselves in a special class that need not try, I believe to that extent we are misleading and misguiding. Education is always the result of individual effort. No child, regardless of how high his IQ, is born educated. He may be born healthy; he may be born bright. But he is not born educated.

The IQ is an empirically determined index. It has certain practical uses for psychologists and counselors in diagnosing pupils and in indicating remedial steps. It lacks a rigorous theoretical foundation, and it presents to the general public, to parents, and to students a grossly oversimplified picture of mental organization. Its widespread use has hampered research into the more significant and more complex types of measurement which we must eventually devise. The relationship between IQ and productivity, even in scholarly fields, is not as high as most people seem to assume. The important matter is what one accomplishes, not how high the IQ, which is chiefly a measure of the speed of learning, but performance. Superior performance is the goal, and, as John Gardner has pointed out in his booklet on *The Pursuit of Excellence*, superior performance is the result of ability, motivation, and character. He goes on to say that in the heat and dust of daily life, the more one observes performance, the more he will be impressed with the contributions of motivation and character. The work of the world (and I am including the scholarly and scientific work) is accomplished by those who have drive and energy directed toward a goal. IQ without motivation is lifeless and useless and, I think, not worthy of the attention which has been directed to it. Personality characteristics which are so important for success are not easily assessed. They may be more important in the final determination, but we do not have means of measuring them yet; consequently, they have largely been ignored.

Let me refer to some of our winners now, because in the long run it is individuals who are the goal of the program of this kind. I thought you might be interested in a few case studies of some of our Negro winners. Selection is made without knowledge of race or religion, and we have had quite a bit of difficulty in determining which ones are Negroes, because we get no such information or photographs from them. One of the Merit winners is a chap who graduated from a segregated school in the Deep South. He is one of a family of three children. His father is a carpenter who did have one year of college; his mother completed the ninth grade.

At this particular school, a parochial school, the student did a distinguished job and was quite active in the various organizations of the school. He ranked first in the school. The priest who is the head of this school described this student as brilliant and quite different from any other student at the school. This boy elected to go from this segregated school in the Deep South to a Midwestern university of distinction. He is majoring in chemistry, which is a difficult subject. A member of the Chess Club there, he also has joined the American Chemistry Society affiliate for students. At the end of his first year he ranked at about the bottom of the top quarter of the class. His counselor writes that he has a somewhat nervous disposition. An aggressive type, he is having some problems in adjusting to the change in his environment. That he should have such problems is to be expected, but that he would rank in the upper quarter of his class is truly astonishing.

Take another case of a young colored girl from Philadelphia. There are two children in the family she comes from. The father has a bachelor's degree, and the mother is a high school graduate. This Merit scholar was the first Negro to be enrolled in a private school in the area where she lives and the first Negro to graduate. In the school, it is interesting to note, she was made a member of the student council, president of the school choir, and vice-president of the senior class. She was taken on a tour of Europe with some of her classmates, and she has done voluntary work in the community's work camps. She ranked in the top 10 percent of the students of this select school. She is going to an East-Coast college, majoring in psychology, and doing outstanding work in mathematics, which is always good for people in psychology to do. Her biology is good, and her literature is fair. She has been elected the president of her dormitory for the next year, a signal honor for any sophomore. Her guidance counselor writes to us that she is eager for knowledge and she is learning to channel her energies to accomplish more.

Another case is a colored boy from the Middle West who has gone to what I would consider a highly superior high school. Both of his parents ended their formal education with graduation from the eighth grade. The father is deceased; the mother is a widow doing domestic work. This chap ranked twentieth in a class of 626, most of whom came from high socioeconomic backgrounds. He was active in the school in outside activities and the editor of the school handbook. Now studying at one of our major institutions in the Midwest, he is majoring in physics. His humanities instructor reported him as one of his most sensitive students. The residence counselor reports that the boy is quite reserved, but apparently well adjusted and happy. He keeps to himself a great deal of the time to permit himself to do more reading. He ranks slightly below the top 10 percent in his class.

Another colored student comes from a segregated high school in Tulsa, Oklahoma, where he ranked first. The parents are college-educated, the father having a master's degree and the mother a bachelor's degree. The boy elected what is considered to be one of the two most difficult engineering institutions in the United States, where he is majoring in electrical engineering. At the end of his first year he was in the top quarter of the class. In addition to being on the dean's list, he was active in intramural sports and is reported to be serious, intelligent, and reliable. These cases demonstrate that we are finding, at this level, students from a racial background that in many cases is deprived.

One of the other aspects of the Merit program should be mentioned. I refer to our research on identification, on the study of environments which are conducive to the development of talents, and on background factors. We are quite convinced that the need, which has been pointed out again and again in this conference, is for very early identification and continuous identification. We need to stimulate the able pupils at an early age and encourage them.

Our work is suggesting that the creative students may not be so well liked or highly recommended by the teachers as the docile, well-behaved, and less creative ones. We also find that most of the colleges are less capable of adapting to the truly creative students so as to make them more productive. Many of our colleges, we find, pay very little attention to the students whom they work so hard to attract—once they have captured them. Some of these students can work with much greater independence than has been granted to them and can advance at much more rapid rates.

Education is the key to our progress both as individuals and as a nation of free people. All of our children will benefit from as much education as their abilities permit. The Merit program strives to help create a climate of opinion in which the public will favor more intellectual training and will honor the disciplined mind. Some progress can be noted. In the words of a distinguished editor, Ordway Tead, the weather is clearing and promises fair.

Discussion Following Mr. Stalnaker's Address

Presiding: LAWRENCE E. DENNIS

DR. BOND: Let me make one or two comments about the program of the National Merit Scholarship Corporation. A great many points have been clarified by Dr. Stalnaker here today, and this has been helpful. The name of the Corporation itself, how-

ever, is likely to lead to a misconception in view of its system of
state quotas, as Mr. Fred M. Hechinger pointed out in his article
in the Sunday *New York Times*. This is unfortunate because the
program has had a tremendous influence on public opinion and,
consequently, on the formulation of legislation.

I think I am right in saying that in awarding scholarships, the
New York State Board of Regents has recognized the fact that the
rural areas are likely to be at a disadvantage and, therefore, has
established rural quotas. This notion of establishing quotas has
been applied to both state and national legislative schemes. If
we are looking for talent on a national scale, it seems to me that
these quotas do a great disservice to the country.

If you plot the National Merit winners by counties throughout
the country, the map shows that even within states you have a
concentration of winners in suburban and upper-class areas. Although I don't know, I suspect that if the National Merit scholarships were awarded on the basis of a national cut-off score, you
would find certain areas, such as suburban Chicago and suburban New York and the Main Line of Philadelphia, receiving
far more than their proportionate share. I suspect that many
states wouldn't get any awards at all, and, from the standpoint of
national policy, I suppose this would be a very good thing if we
are looking for the brightest of all in the entire nation.

The whole basic theory of "talent" (that is, what it is) has been
interpreted here to mean "developed scholastic ability." The historical connotation of this concept seems to me to need examination.

For this very reason, I have frequently wished that the data of
the National Merit Scholarship Corporation could be published or
made available in greater detail for the inspection, use, and interpretation of persons interested in the subject because of the
gravity of this situation. I have the feeling that programs of this
sort have had the dangerous effect of distracting attention from
the needs of schools for the masses and of encouraging what may
be a false notion in the minds of the American public with reference to the origin of human ability. If we are engaged in discovering native ability, should we focus almost exclusively on

developed scholastic ability among the upper crust or on the tremendous needs of large-scale populations such as those involved in Project 43, described by Mr. Plaut?

This is the point that seems to me to be of extreme importance. We need to study the whole question of social mobility. Do we have as much of it as we think we have in this country? What are its implications for our whole democracy in planning education? These considerations have led me to a deep interest in the study of the social sources of scholars and to the hope that more useful data would be made available.

If I have been either scurrilous or impudent in regard to these matters, I do apologize to Dr. Stalnaker. My interest in this problem goes back to the time when he was with the Association of Medical Colleges and when he was concerned with the testing procedures there for minority groups. I want to quote one statement in the book by D. C. Reitzes, *Negroes and Medicine:* [1]

Scores on these tests (i.e., Medical College Admissions Tests) for candidates educated outside the United States should be interpreted with considerable caution. While the caution is self-evident in the case of foreign-language-speaking students, it applies also to English-speaking students educated outside the United States. For them a negative bias may be expected on the test in Understanding Modern Society, since it is based principally on issues of contemporary interest in the United States.

As I pointed out in reviewing this book for the *Journal of Negro Education*, [2] it seems to me that the problem of the Negroes, Puerto Ricans, and other minority groups is that of people who are foreigners to the main stream of the standard American culture. They are speaking a "foreign language" from the standpoint of their cultural context which is alien to the standard American culture. I was glad, Dr. Stalnaker, to hear you say what you did about the implications of the IQ. I would hope that research would be directed to the point of identifying talented persons who come from a foreign-language area (which is where Negroes and Puerto Ricans in our big cities come from). We need to work

[1] Published for the Commonwealth Fund; Cambridge, Mass.: Harvard University Press, 1958. P. 377.
[2] Spring 1959.

out devices which realistically weight test scores. I do not distrust test scores; I think they are wonderful things. I do hope, however, that research may be directed to the point where, in a low-scoring population, we can use test results balanced against socioeconomic background to come out with a true index of ability.

Excuse me for this long-winded statement. I have to leave immediately, and I don't want to leave without expressing my profound appreciation for Dr. Stalnaker's leadership of the National Merit Scholarship Corporation and for the remarks he made here this morning. They highlight an attitude I think we all need to develop with reference to the implications of tests.

MR. STALNAKER: I appreciate the cogent and well-phrased remarks that Dr. Bond has made. In responding to his several points, I would like to make clear at the outset that I think any agency, such as National Merit, should be subjected to constant criticism. Please do not conclude that because I enjoy answering comments which have been made, the criticism is unwelcome. We should have more reasoned criticism than we are getting, not less.

The first point you raised concerns the state quotas. Would the influence we are having be enhanced if we made all selections on a national basis? This point is a controversial one. My judgment is that what we are now doing has a better influence than would using a national cutting score. We select our semifinalists on a state basis, in ratio to the number of high school graduates in the last year for which statistics are available. We then issue on a national basis—and without reference to state quotas—letters of commendation to 27,500 students. In some states, no students receive letters of commendation; hence the influence of this phase of the program is zero in those states. In one state, more than 5,000 students received letters of commendation this year.

The dual system of recognizing regional differences and acknowledging the state as the proper unit on the one hand and the national selection of the commended group on the other produces results which we believe are helpful to all sections of the country. We do not want to rule out any state, because a student can be superior eventually in spite of the limitations of his schooling over which he had no control. In our first year, the lowest-scoring Merit scholar, selected from a location not known for its superior secondary schools, entered one of our most popular prestige colleges and has now graduated in less than four years with a distinguished record. The question of state or national selection is an open one. If we can marshal evidence to support a shift from our present method and if the evidence convinces the controlling group, then we shall change. I am not persuaded at the moment that we should change from our present dual system, but I am sure we can make some improvements in the details of the system, and we are working on these now.

The second point you made concerned the influence of social standing. You suggested that we should not allow illustrations of exceptions to distort the main picture, and I agree with you in general. We agree that social mobility does exist, and I think our quibble, if any, would concern the extent to which it exists, the breadth of the channel of mobility, and how high one can move in a generation. I would grant that these are very important matters. We want to operate the Merit program so that it encourages and facilitates social mobility. We are now getting some students from the low socioeconomic groups, and I find this comforting even though, percentagewise, it is small.

The third point you raised concerned the problem of defining "talent." I agree fully with what you said. At the present time, in most conferences like this, talent is equated to a score on a test. Theoretically at least, one could say that talented persons are those who have purpose, direction, ambition, and energy, as well as ability. In other words, the definition should include certain important characteristics in addition to the abilities reflected in a test score. Because the test score is a very precise figure and the other characteristics cannot be accurately measured at this time, we tend to stress the test score. I agree thoroughly that talent should be defined somewhat differently than it now is.

Your fourth point concerned publishing in greater detail the data which we have. The only information that we have been a bit "cozy" about has been the cutting scores for the various states. We will give these to any person who has legitimate use for them.

There is no secret about them. The cutting scores for the states show what any person who has examined other national test data already knows. The students in the Deep South, on the average, do not score as high as the students in New York or Illinois. However, there are very superior students in every state. We feel that, with the present intense public interest, the publication of our figures would result in national attention being focused on "the best" state and "the worst" state. What would the benefit be? But maybe we have to go through a phase where this is done. The Selective Service test data on state differences have been published. Some of the Army data have shown the same results. The only reason we don't publish other data in more complete detail is the sheer expense of doing so. Nobody has been refused any information he has asked for. I can't say that we won't some day refuse, because there is the problem of taking care of such requests. We cannot go to great expense to supply everyone with requested information, but we are maintaining our data for public benefit.

Your final point concerns the extent to which a program like this detracts or diverts attention from the education of the masses. Obviously, we should be concerned with all our children and not limit our attention to any selected group of children. I would argue here (perhaps as a salesman for the Merit program) that to date the most neglected student in our school system has been the able student. It is time to focus a little more attention on him. This is true in colleges as well as in secondary schools. I agree that the attention focused on very able students can become too great and, therefore, divert us from other important interests. When this comes about, various forces will reorient our interests in other directions. Right now, however, we need to give more attention to intellectual development, to its values, to the needs for it, and to ways of fostering it. By concentrating on the very best, we can help to bring about this desired result.

FREDERICK C. COPELAND (Director of Admissions, Williams College): Dr. Stalnaker, since the eventual winners, as well as the 10,000 semifinalists, are picked solely on the results of an examination, I am wondering whether or not you have made any analysis of the background of this 10,000 or of the 27,000 who scored over 134. These are all extremely capable boys and girls who rate very high in their age group in terms of intellectual ability. It seems to me an analysis of their backgrounds would be very significant.

DR. STALNAKER: We are making an analysis of this group. We are making an analysis of where they are going to college, an analysis of what they are studying, and some analysis of their financial and social backgrounds, as well as an analysis of types of schools that they come from. All of these matters are much more complicated than they seem to be when you merely mention them. It is very easy to suggest a study of this kind, but it is very tough to do it, as I am sure Jack Darley will attest. But we are making a little headway.

Although we have been given some money by the National Science Foundation and the Old Dominion Foundation, we find it very difficult, in general, to get money for "free" research, as opposed to restricted research. I am not anxious to try to do too much research. This type of research has to be decentralized and done in many, many locations. But I would like to make a plea that more money be given for more free research in this area.

FATHER SMITH: Dr. Stalnaker, I have wondered since the beginning of the National Merit Scholarship program whether or not there would be full participation on the part of all the school systems. In the four or five years the program has been operating, have you noticed an increase in the participation or do some schools hold out?

DR. STALNAKER: There has been an increase in participation every year, both in the number of schools and in the number of students. The distribution of schools in this country includes a very large number of extremely small schools and schools in very deprived areas. These are the most difficult schools to interest in a program of this kind and, I daresay, any other kind. They don't have graduates who go to college; they are inadequately and, usually, poorly staffed. It is quite a tough problem to get through to these schools.

Participation is less in the deprived areas and in the segregated schools of the South. We are doing all we can, but we are a voluntary organization. No one needs to participate if he doesn't want to. All we can do is invite and urge. I don't have the information that I would like very much to have and that I wish I could obtain, but I would guess that the schools participating in our program probably enroll 85 or 90 percent of the high school population. I don't know this; I am merely guessing. My guess is, however, that our 14,500 schools include 85 or 90 percent of the population. I am not sure how much higher than that we can hope to go. Even in the days of the Army-Navy College Qualifying Test, if I remember correctly, we didn't enroll much more than 14,000 to 15,000 schools, and this was a program of advantage to every male in the United States. I think it will be difficult to go very much higher than we have, but we are striving to do so.

Miss Paschal: Mr. Stalnaker, would you care to comment on what your problems would be if, instead of requiring enrollments of the schools, you permitted some applications from individual students.

Dr. Stalnaker: The problem here would be to distribute the information to these individuals. If the school does not tell the students about the existence of the program, they won't know about it. If any student should write to us and say, "I want to participate in this program very much, but my school will not have anything to do with it," we would allow the student to register. Thus far in the program, we have not had a half dozen cases of this kind. From an administrative point of view, it would be very, very difficult for us to deal directly with the students on a large scale.

Mr. Plaut: How would you test a student who got in touch with you directly?

Dr. Stalnaker: We would direct him to a participating school nearby. That is what we have done.

Mr. Moon: John, I believe you said that your ratio of males to females in the finalist group is 3 to 1. We have learned the last few days that about an equal number of males and females graduate from the very-high-ability groups in the high schools but that the greatest talent loss from high school to college is among the women. It seems to me that your program, in maintaining this ratio, is contributing to this unbalanced situation rather than helping it. Is this just the way the test comes out or are the results some way manipulated to produce this ratio?

DR. STALNAKER: We do not wish to contribute to the downfall of women, I assure you. We do not manipulate anything to cause this, other than to administer the initial test. Since the initial test has quantitative as well as verbal material in it, one could say that this is in itself a manipulation. In our cultural pattern, it is not "smart" for girls to learn mathematics. This is not the way they endear themselves to their boy friends, I am told. As a result, the girls fall down at this very top level in a material way. No other kind of "manipulation" than the basic test enters into this.

Again, I will make a diversionary move here and say that some of the girls whom we have selected have been magnificent mathematicians. In one college of mining and engineering, which dislikes having any girls at all, we have a girl who is leading her class and who has done so ever since she has been there. This is a great trial to the institution, and I am sure her life is going to be tough.

DR. LITTLE: Do more girls than boys take the test?

DR. STALNAKER: Slightly more.

MELVENE D. HARDEE (Professor, School of Education, Florida State University): I was interested in your remarks that we put more emphasis on talent identification than on what happens to the student in college. Do most Merit scholars have access to a full-time, trained counselor or a faculty adviser? Do you differentiate?

DR. STALNAKER: We do not differentiate in that way, and I do not know. It is always dangerous to make comments about what goes on in any college. As far as the Merit program is concerned, we have great respect for the superior job that most colleges are doing. However, some colleges do better than others. We received a notice from one college that the student had left. Naturally, this disturbed us and, after about a week's telephoning, we found out that the student was really there, but that the college didn't know that he was there. There are a number of colleges that do not know that students are there. It is difficult to get very meaningful reports from them. Of course, those are exceptions, and most of the colleges are doing a wonderful job.

Dr. Wolfle: Can a student combine the advantages of a Merit scholarship and early admission? Do you have any provision for the ones who want to make the transition to college earlier than usual?

Dr. Stalnaker: We now admit into the program any student who is recommended by his high school as ready for college and acceptable to a college. There are some problems in scheduling and timing. A person must take the test a little over a year in advance of the time he wants to enter college. He may be technically classified as a sophomore or freshman at that time. We don't care. If the high school recommends him and the college accepts him, he would be eligible for a Merit scholarship.

Lucile Allen (Consultant, Austin College): Would it be wise for counselors in secondary schools to suggest to students who are interested in trying out for this program that four years of mathematics and four years of science would be the best way of preparing for it?

Dr. Stalnaker: No, ma'am, I do not think this is what should be done. I will be pious here. I think that the secondary schools should decide what kind of a curriculum is best for able students. I would hope that the curriculum would include the "solid-subject-matter" fields: English, history, mathematics, science, and foreign language. But I think these subjects should be recommended because *the school* believes they are what the student should study and not because studying them will help him earn a Merit scholarship. The chance of any student getting a Merit scholarship is very, very small.

Mr. Jackson: John, I have two questions: First, how accurate do you think the examinations in this very rarefied range are? Second, do you see any chance of developing reliable techniques to measure other very important factors, such as motivation, so that they can be considered in the selection process?

Dr. Stalnaker: To answer the first question, I think the test is doing quite an adequate job in the upper range. If I confess to anything, I confess that I am worried about how effective these tests are because that goes against some of the other theories that I dearly love.

In answer to the second question, we are doing a good deal of research on other characteristics but, thus far, most of the measures do not lend themselves to use in a pressure situation. They lend themselves to use much better in a situation where the student wants to cooperate and reveal rather than to conceal and distort. When one is in a competition to gain the top, he does what he thinks he needs to do to get to the top. This is not the kind of situation in which you can ask the questions that furnish information about his personality. So, while we are doing research, I am not optimistic about any early breakthrough. Jack Darley would probably like to comment on this from his point of view.

DR. DARLEY: I would agree with what you say. There are certain devices that cannot be used in the situation you describe.

Dr. Stalnaker's staff is doing good research on nonintellectual variables. With their cooperation, we were able to get some significant personality information on the winners in 1956 and on a 10 percent sample of the runners-up. We are finding quite clear relationships between six or seven personality variables and the types of institutions and curricula chosen. Breakthroughs are coming, but the information will not be helpful in the pressure situation. The place where many of these variables can be considered will be at the point of selection from among the group by panels of experts with experience in socioeconomic backgrounds.

DR. VROMAN: I have a gnawing question on my mind. I have been on the National Merit scholarship selection team, and I am very familiar with its selection program. This program consists entirely of youngsters who are ready and able to compete by all the ground rules for superior students. But how do we work with the disadvantaged youth who may have the potential but who isn't prepared academically to survive this extremely vigorous competition at the top? How do admissions officers, like myself, recognize a really talented but disadvantaged youth who looks like just another mediocre student when he submits his application for admission? Therein lies the challenge of this meeting. The major question is how do we get a disadvantaged student across the threshold into college if we use only our standard measures to analyze that student and his readiness for college? If you look over a hundred applications for admission, the disadvantaged person will look no different to you than the poor students who have not been motivated. This is the problem that challenges us.

Miss TANNEYHILL: May I make some practical suggestions of what we need to do in order to *create the climate* in which personal incentive can be developed? I think we need to:

1. Assemble the facts and make them known to institutions of higher education, to boards of education, superintendents of schools, and others in key positions within our educational system;

2. Gather information on programs and activities that are presently directed at this problem and disseminate this information as widely as possible so others can go forth to do likewise;

3. Look at our existing research to see if it will give clues to new programs that can be undertaken;

4. Make extended use of *all* of the media of mass communication—newspapers, popular magazines, filmslides, filmstrips, radio, TV, even the lowly comic book—to reach and inform teachers, counselors, parents, and organizations that come in contact with mothers and fathers and with young people themselves. As Mr. Gardner so well states in the little leaflet we have all read, "Any adequate attack on this problem will reach far beyond formal educational institutions. It will involve not only the school, but the home, the church, the playground, and all of the institutions which shape the individual. . . . Unions, lodges, professional organizations, and social clubs can all contribute importantly to individual growth and learning if they are so inclined."

5. *Finally,* make serious efforts to persuade the Advertising Council to adopt a program of five-year duration to convince the American public that the identification, development, and utilization of the talents of *all* of its youth is a great national concern and, in a democracy, our most important business.

MR. JACKSON: In two or three of the presentations that were made yesterday and today, the remark was made that we know how to identify disadvantaged students, but we are not so sure what to do with them. This leads me to put in a plug for more demonstration projects. We had descriptions of at least two here yesterday, the project in Junior High 43 and Washington High School in New York and the project involving a hundred high schools in the North Central Association of Colleges and Secondary Schools. These barely scratch the surface. There is nothing in the South or the West that I know of.

It seems to me that we need a lot of activity in this area, and I think that this calls for people simply sitting down and putting their minds to work on this problem to see what they can figure out. I have seen this work in the improvement of the teaching of mathematics. A little group at the University of Illinois, a little group at the University of Maryland, and another group working under the aegis of the College Board have done a lot to change and upgrade the whole mathematics curriculum in the elementary and secondary schools.

It seems to me a lot more can be done in this area of encouraging disadvantaged youth. Then, somewhere along the line, it seems to me that the programs under way need to be evaluated by outsiders who are not connected with them so that the best practices can be publicized nationally.

DR. THEOBALD: If we assume that we can easily identify the potentially talented youngster, we are making a terrible mistake. The talented child in the second or third grade who comes from a totally different kind of culture, a culture that misses half of the things that we assume are standard in every child's background, can't be identified easily. If he is not identified, he not only doesn't develop his potential, but frequently becomes a drag on society later. Our number one problem is to develop better means of early identification of ability in the youngster who doesn't follow the normal cultural pattern.

MR. PLAUT: I couldn't agree with Dr. Theobald more.

MR. SHULMAN: I have been waiting for this part of the program to learn how all the research that has been done on the identification and motivation of such students would be translated into practical measures. We are always on the alert for new and more effective means of reaching these children and their parents. This is the number one problem. We have used all the customary methods—the mails, phone calls, and visits to the home, and we have not found them entirely satisfactory.

On occasion, we pay a surprise visit to the parent at his place of employment. While he may be annoyed by our visit, he is also embarrassed. He may not be in awe of school authorities, but he is concerned about his employer's reaction to our presence. Our being there gets across to the parent the urgency of the problem. And to keep us from coming again, he will cooperate a little more fully.

Not only must we reach these parents, we must stimulate them, too. It is difficult for a youngster to develop an interest in the drama, music, or art when the parent is uninformed or even critical of such recreational pursuits. Some parents even object to their children's attendance at school. One father repeatedly said, "Why do you waste your time going to school? When I was your age, I was self-supporting."

We try to provide for the development and expression of students' interests and aptitudes. This has helped to modify some antisocial behavior. One boy, who had a compulsion for writing pornographic notes and stories, was programmed for a class in creative writing. He came to like the class so well that the teacher was able to interest him in submitting poems and stories to student publications. He later had the satisfaction of seeing several of his contributions appear in an anthology of high school poetry.

To help them acquire personal satisfaction and social competence, we encourage their participation in dramatic, musical, athletic, and service activities, both in school and the community. Some of our girls serve as nurses' aides; some of the boys are leaders-in-training at recreation centers. Thus they learn about possible careers while getting the personal satisfaction of performing a worthwhile service.

It is important to have continuity in the stimulation of these children. There are many gaps, the summer vacation being a long one. Even a Christmas or Easter vacation threatens the desirable influences we try to provide for these children. Perhaps some way can be found to provide cultural and recreational activities on a full-time basis. The project students need extra time to make up for their educational disabilities. That is why I urge everybody to attend summer school to repeat or advance in academic work. If they are unable to attend summer school, students are urged to borrow one or more textbooks in subjects they will be studying in the fall. This advance preparation will provide a general background of information which will make the course easier and pleasanter. We try to encourage them to pursue cultural activities independently. We mention all the places of interest that can be visited at low cost or free of charge.

Mr. Schreiber: I think that we need to bear in mind what one can do to a group by one's attitude toward the group. If a person who is in a position of authority feels that a group is incapable of doing good work, this feeling is transmitted to the group. After a while, the group not only feels that it is incapable of doing good work but actually does poor work.

The implication of this is that we must direct our attention to teacher attitudes toward children. As teachers, we must really believe in the dignity of all people, especially people who are superficially different from us because of color, race, or religion. Unless we accept this simple belief and treat all children as "our" children, we will make it difficult for disadvantaged children to rise above the level of their parents.

I think that the best thing this group can do is to help change teachers' attitudes towards children from disadvantaged homes. Until we do that, nothing else will matter.

Many disadvantaged children in New York City come from motherless or fatherless homes. The fatherless home is more predominant. I would like to see in our own city a group of men who would become auxiliary fathers to boys from fatherless homes. If a fatherless boy has someone with whom to watch a ball game, bowl, play football, or just talk to, he will then have a new image in his life—a model to follow and a man to emulate. I have a sneaking suspicion that many boys join gangs in order to gain male experiences. This program cannot be left to happenstance but should be organized by a community agency such as a YMCA. It would be necessary to pair the right boy with the right father. Resource persons, such as counselors, psychologists, and psychiatrists, should be available so that the auxiliary father may go to them for advice and help. If need be, he may refer the boy to them.

I think that we in education have omitted a vital motivating factor in the lives of our children. We may have been unduly influenced by recent biographies of our national heroes. Woodward's biography of George Washington in the forties seems to have set the pattern of stressing the "feet of clay" rather than the accomplishments. Our children need models on which to pattern their lives. These models need not be superior ones. They may be just older persons who care about them and help them raise their sights.

I remember reading only recently an article by an anthropologist who claimed that the Russian leaders knew exactly what they were doing when they made claims that a Russian invented the electric bulb, the automobile, and the telephone. In America, we laughed at these claims because we knew they were not true. I feel quite certain that the Russian leaders knew this, too. But they were creating a "model" in the minds of Russian youth; they were saying to the Russian boy and girl, who had no means of discovering whether the statements were true or false: "A Russian was able to create and to discover. You are a Russian; therefore, you, too, can do the same thing." Surely, we can provide our children with honest models that provide real hope and inspiration.

Mr. Herbert L. Wright: I think it is very important to provide "models" for disadvantaged youth, but I think it is equally important that we make sure they are *meaningful* models, models with which a boy or girl can personally identify himself or herself. There are many ways in which this might be done.

I have had the privilege of participating in many "career-day" programs sponsored by school boards and private agencies around the country. I think that these programs have not been as effective as they might have been for minority groups simply because most of the participants have been white. Even if the guidance counselor says, "Any one of you can aspire to this kind of career," the minority youth tends to take it with a grain of salt and say to himself, "This is not open to me." The impact of these programs on minority youth would be much greater if the participants or "models" were themselves members of the minority group to which they are speaking.

In addition to providing models, we need to provide much better information concerning opportunities for scholarships in higher education and opportunities for employment in various fields that are now opening up to minority groups. Up-to-date information of this kind will also help to motivate youngsters, for it will give them assurance that it is possible to move upward and to aspire to something worthwhile.

CHAIRMAN DENNIS: There is a phrase directed to this point in the statement of purpose of this conference: "Whereas able young people influenced toward higher education by favorable environments develop drives sufficient to overcome formidable obstacles, those not so fortunately influenced seldom understand opportunities that are theirs. What they do not understand, they do not value; what they do not value, they do not pursue."

I think we have time for two more comments.

MISS PASCHAL: I would like to go back to something that our keynote speaker said. I think we have lost sight of the fact that one of the most effective ways of holding a youngster in school and of motivating him for college is to provide a really stimulating educational experience. I think the lack of intellectual stimulation which often comes from poor teaching and an uninspiring curriculum causes many students to fail, to become discouraged, and to drop out.

MR. MOON: I want to make eight observations which may summarize many of the things we have talked about here:

1. Preparation for post-high-school education must again become an important function of the public schools; however, it must be achieved under an entirely different set of social and intellectual conditions than prevailed before World War I.

2. It is essential that education at all levels be provided in an atmosphere that emphasizes the worth of the individual.

3. The methods by which the intellectual potentialities of young people are now evaluated need to be extensively re-examined.

4. Likewise, the nonintellectual aspects of personality and their relationship to the individual's educational progress need to be seriously studied.
5. We should realize that progress in developing better incentives for higher education may be slow from now on since the "hunting" actually has been heavy in the most productive areas in recent years.
6. The success of efforts to increase personal incentives for education at all levels should not be judged solely by quantitative changes in college-going but by qualitative ones as well.
7. No one kind of post-high-school educational system will assure the maximum utilization of our talented youth.
8. Steps should be immediately undertaken by higher education to assure the full development of personal incentive for higher education, but such steps should reflect broad public responsibility. Education alone has not caused this problem; education alone cannot solve it.

Next Steps in Encouraging Personal Incentive among Talented but Disadvantaged Youth

FRANK H. BOWLES

President, College Entrance Examination Board

As I MAKE THESE CONCLUDING REMARKS, I SHALL NECESSARILY BE repeating, in the interest of re-emphasis, certain of the salient points which have been made in the course of the conference. My primary concern is to offer some commentary on the present status of our talented but disadvantaged youth, and then to speculate on what should or might be some logical next steps.

The problem is certainly not a new one. It has been with us throughout the twentieth century, though its presence has perhaps been felt more acutely during periods of wartime and depression. In 1900, only five or six percent of the college-age group went on to higher education, and the high school itself was in fact largely a college-preparatory institution. Now, after over a half century of growth and development, half of all our high school graduates go on to some type of higher education.

During World War II, we began to discover the real dimensions of the talent problem. We could not find enough college-trained persons to do the jobs which called for higher education. After the war, veterans went to college in great numbers with the assistance of the GI bill of rights. In the course of the next two decades our system of secondary education has doubled, and higher education has experienced a parallel expansion.

What is the problem we are dealing with today? How do we state it? As originally stated about ten years ago, it went something like this: "About one-half of the top 25 percent of the nation's most able students do not go on to higher education." This remains the basic statement. It continues to be discussed, but it is rarely amplified with clarity. I heard it presented as a new observation at an educational meeting only last summer. Can we now state the problem in more specific terms?

Until recently, we were not able even to describe the kind of person who, in effect, fails to be developed. I well remember when the College Board was asked by the National Science Foundation to undertake the study which ended up with the title *Encouraging Scientific Talent*. We floundered for days asking ourselves, "How do you describe scientific talent? How do you encourage it when you don't know what it is?" It was an undefined problem then, and it has remained undefined until most recently. Only within the last few years have we realized that when we talk about undeveloped talent, we are actually talking about three groups of people: First, we are talking about people of known academic ability that has not been developed to its full capacity. Second, we are talking about people who have creative talents but who do not show up in the academically superior group. Then, finally, we are talking about people who have "submerged" talent. It has been particularly interesting in this conference to notice the number of times we have referred to "the problem of submerged talents." It is a good indication that we have made some progress in defining the problem and in analyzing its parts. This is an auspicious beginning.

Much of our knowledge of talent rests upon a very narrow base. There is Dael Wolfle's pioneering work.[1] There is Byron Hollinshead's book,[2] which relied largely on Wolfle's data. There is the National Science Foundation–College Board–ETS set of studies which eventuated in the study of high school seniors and their motivation for college. There is Charles Cole's book, *Encouraging Scientific Talent*, which was published by the College Board. And there is the National Merit program. Others are coming along now, but they are still few in number.

We have come a good deal closer to observing the true dimen-

[1] *America's Resources of Specialized Talent* (New York: Harper & Bros., 1954).
[2] *Who Should Go to College* (New York: Columbia University Press, 1954).

sions of one part of the problem, the dimensions of academic potential. We still do not know—and I want to emphasize this— we still know almost nothing about the identification of creative talent. We still know very little about the identification of submerged talent. But at least we are beginning to get descriptions which help solve the problem of people of recognizable ability who have the opportunity and who clearly have the potential to develop further.

We do know that certain conditions affect the whole range of ability. For example, one of the factors often found among students who have low aspirations and who have not developed their talent to the fullest is segregation for racial, national, or economic reasons. Negroes and the Puerto Ricans suffer from this blight. So do some members of the working class that lives across the tracks or, in the modern parlance, that lives on the other side of the superhighway. So do some groups that live in nondescript and older parts of great cities or in depressed areas that cover whole communities or whole regions.

We know very little about these groups. We don't even know how many people are involved. I doubt if anyone does. But let's assume that the number might be as much as 10 percent of the population, and it might even be more. That would be a lot of people.

I heard reference this morning to the "problem of bicultural affinity," to the problem of Negroes and Puerto Ricans who actually live in two cultures in cities like New York. In the feudal and agricultural part of our South, both whites and Negroes live in bicultural situations. The language and culture they experience at home is a different culture than the one they experience in school and in the larger community.

There are, of course, many other factors affecting those who do not realize their potential and who do not wish to realize their potential. Dr. Havighurst mentioned one last week in New York when he discussed the problem of achieving adult status. That is another problem relating to the group we are talking about. The pressure upon the students of potential ability to achieve adult status has been a mark of development within their family structure or their culture. Very often, they must actually go against family traditions in order to move forward into the academic role that we would like to have them assume. Thus, their group membership produces socially induced frustrations which press in on them. They encounter the physical restraint of environment, the family restraint of custom, and the intellectual restraint of segregated and lower-quality schools.

One of our special problems is that these groups are very difficult to test. Many of our conventional testing instruments fail to measure the potential of these students. Someone said this morning that he doesn't think the intelligence test is an adequate device and that he deplored its use. I don't know that I would deplore its use. The IQ has been one of the concepts by which we have been able to communicate the idea of intelligence and of ability levels. But I do deplore the notion that an individual's IQ is fixed. Dan Schreiber has described the boy who is presently leading his class at George Washington High School and who left Junior High School 43 with an IQ of 115. I suppose it is possible that a boy with this IQ could be leading the class, but I think it is very unlikely considering the competitive nature of that group. I think an accurate measurement of this student's ability would probably be much higher.

We could say more about this problem of testing. It has been a serious problem, and it is one which the testing agencies have only begun to examine. But I want to move on to another topic. I have already said that expansion of education has actually swallowed up many of the problems we thought we had, and I have suggested the normal expansion of American education may possibly alleviate some of the problems which we have discussed today. For example, the rise in real income of the lower classes has certainly gone a long way toward ameliorating part of the talent problem. Another promising trend is the progress we are making toward the goal of a national testing and scholarship program that we set up about ten years ago.

Last spring, as John Stalnaker said, the National Merit program tested 550,000 eleventh-graders. Two weeks ago, the College Board tested about 630,000 eleventh-graders. I don't know how many the Merit program will test in the spring, but let's assume it will test somewhere around this number. Even if there is a very large overlap, we are getting very close to a national testing program of real size and importance. When we arrive at a point where we are testing a million eleventh-graders, we are really getting close to finding out what the ability levels are. So we are making progress on the testing problem.

Ten years ago, we realized we needed a national scholarship program, and we now have the National Merit program. It is not as large as it should be and does not cover as many levels as it might; nevertheless, it is a very significant program and, of course, an essential part of the national testing program. In the last decade, in many ways, we have opened the doors of college to students who thought they could never get there. Many students who a few years ago would not have dreamed of going to college now believe they can get to college.

As a result of these changes, we have had more success than we can use in some ways. The public relations approach to the talent search involves four steps: identification, counseling, scholarships, and enrollment. We have an identification program with counseling fairly well built into it so that we can depend on a fair degree of motivation on the part of the one million eleventh-graders. However, we know that there will not be scholarships enough to go around, not nearly enough. Furthermore, there won't be enough places in college to meet the requirements of this group.

Let me elaborate a bit. There are in the country approximately 100 "elite" colleges that are considered most desirable and that are the goal of students who are highly motivated with respect to higher education. Let us be generous and assume that they have among them a freshman class of 100,000 students. These colleges now have at least 250,000 candidates for these 100,000 places. What are we going to do with the 150,000 who were particularly motivated to go to these colleges, partly through our efforts, and who now can't get there? Suppose we double the effectiveness of our program. Then what are we going to do, not with 150,000 who can't get in but with 400,000 who cannot find spaces in these 100,000 vacancies?

As we consider such comprehensive issues, it appears that our public relations operation may actually have begun to reach the point of diminishing returns. Colleges are no longer able to meet the requirements of all the students who come to them. The public relations have been so successful that it is now time to consider whether we can continue the present level of public relations activities with our present physical resources. I have a relevant and frightening story to illustrate.

As a Columbia University alumnus, I am a member of an alumni committee which is supposed to keep the college in touch with its alumni body. We meet monthly. About three weeks ago when the committee met, I was asked to introduce the present director of admissions, Joe Jefferson, and his new colleague, Dave Dudley, and to discuss their work in the area of admissions. On this occasion I was perhaps more eloquent than usual about Columbia and about the things it has done and the things it can do. I alluded to the Pulitzer scholarships, the oldest major scholarship program of its size and style in the country and one of the very best. I spoke of Junior High School 43, which is Columbia's own junior high school, as well as the College Board's. I spoke of Glyn Morris and his guidance activities in the coal country, of the Catskill group that attempts to give college guidance, and of the Rocky Mountain project for a similar group of small high schools. After my colleagues talked, we all sat back well satisfied with ourselves.

Immediately, a couple of alumni got up and lambasted us all over the lot. Why, they asked, are you wasting the university's time and money on futile idealism in the pursuit of the few students who may qualify and who won't even be gentlemen? This very strong critical reaction seemed to come not just from a man or two, but, I felt, from the whole group of alumni, all of whom I consider to be literate and intelligent. The feeling seemed to be that the university admissions office was not doing its job when it spent time on this problem; the consensus seemed to be that it was the job of the admissions people to attract the qualified students with money, thus enabling Columbia to save its scholarship resources to recruit a football team (which, heaven knows, it needs) and to do various other things of this type.

Well, it was disillusioning, of course. But I don't tell this story to explain my disappointment; I tell it to point out that even well-intentioned and, apparently, well-educated people do not understand this problem. Nor do they understand the obligation of universities to do something about it. Our public relations should take still another factor into account, if we want to avoid raising hopes that cannot be fulfilled. It seems quite abundantly clear that the great educational problem with which our secondary schools must deal over the next twenty years is the raising of academic standards for college preparation by the equivalent of one full year. I think this is going to have to be done without increasing the length of the secondary school course and without decreasing the length of the college course. In other words, I think there is a year's slack which could now be taken up. There are a number of colleges now whose advanced placement requirements represent the difference of one academic year from the mean achievement of high school graduates in the country. As entrance standards begin to climb through the stiffer selection forced by numbers, I believe the number of colleges operating on what are, in effect, super-entrance requirements will increase. I doubt if it is going to go beyond one hundred to two hundred colleges, but, even at that, it will affect probably one-half of American college-going students. This is a pretty sizable segment of the educational population.

If superior students are to be identified and encouraged to go to college, we should make certain that there are enough qualified teachers to go around. This isn't the case at the present time with respect to the best students and the best colleges; moreover, there is some doubt as to whether it is going to be the case for lower-level students and lower-level colleges later on. In other words, the expansion of higher education commensurate with the contemplated increase of superior students is not proceeding very well.

We had better make certain, too, that the standard secondary school program meets the standard college program and that the best secondary school programs are on a par with the best college programs. If this is not done, there will be a great deal of waste motion and disappointment. Some of the benefits of encouragement are already being lost in classrooms. Schools and colleges must continue their present interesting but limited programs relating to advanced placement. These could be increased tenfold and still affect only small numbers of secondary school students. If increased tenfold, however, they would have quite an effect on secondary schools.

As far as the curriculum is concerned, much needs to be done to provide for the needs of students whose talents are of a different order from those who show high promise. Thus, a vocational, a semiprofessional or an average-quality liberal arts program made available to average students who would otherwise have no opportunities to go to college, might well prove to be a major contribution to the nation, even though the contribution may not be noticeable within this generation. To put it another way, I think that education of average quality may make a very great contribution merely by providing a succeeding generation with parents who have had a minimal but satisfactory experience with education.

It might well be that the investment within a community of $100,000 in scholarships would produce within a few years a small number of well-educated persons of superior ability; however, the investment of a like amount in a community college might produce more individuals per year educated to modest attainments who, over a generation, could establish a higher cultural level in the community and make it a better place to live.

These are some of the conventional steps that we might take. What unconventional steps might be taken in this area? Suppose we established a national commission and clearinghouse on talent to collect data, coordinate projects, direct research, and provide information. This would certainly be a step forward. I see no reason why there could not be a National Talent Foundation as there was a National Infantile Paralysis Foundation.

We could follow John Monro's suggestion to pool college resources for recruiting and for the study of important problems. Why does this suggestion not gain any ground? I suspect it is because too many college admissions officers are afraid that if some other college admissions officer went to a given high school, he might get a student for his college instead of—well, you see what I am saying. There is so much competition in colleges for superior students that, even though many of them have all the students they can use, they are still reluctant to let anyone else have a chance that they don't have. I really think it is shameful that we have not pooled these resources. There is so much time wasted in going to "college days," in sending 60 admissions officers to a College Day that 10 admissions officers could handle adequately. Since they all know each other's spiels, we could put this concentrated talent to better use and spread a good deal more of the word around the country.

Another idea I might present is this: Colleges could turn some of their scholarships over to the National Merit Scholarship Corporation. This is a professional organization awarding scholarships on the basis of merit. Colleges complain about the difficulty of getting their scholarships to stick. They complain about the number of scholarships and awards they have to offer in order to get the students they want. Some of this could be handled through the Merit Corporation.

These are the specific suggestions that I think I have, but I would like to make a more general one. What would we do about this problem if we could begin all over again next September with an absolutely clean slate and with adequate resources?

We could start at a very early age to test and observe. If we were calm about it, didn't push, and just observed, we would begin to develop our school programs in terms of appropriate studies and extracurricular activities. We could begin college preparation at the seventh grade, where it is going to commence by and by. We could begin to concentrate on counseling and guidance at the seventh grade instead of waiting, as we now do, for the eleventh grade. (It has taken ten years to extend counseling from the twelfth grade to the eleventh grade; so it will take us quite a long time to get to the seventh grade; however, if we were starting all over again, this would be the place to start!)

Ideally, we should remove the question of financial ability. I know of one institution that does this now. It admits its class and then finds out what scholarships are needed. If we can remove the problem of financial ability (and can do it honestly), we would go far toward dealing with the problem.

We could train faculty members and counselors to realize that all academic performance is symptomatic of personality. Nowadays when we find an "over-achiever," we think this is wonderful; when we get an "under-achiever," we think something is wrong. Both of these are examples of personality conflicts. It seems to me that normal academic performance is considered something of an aberration.

All this adds up to better schools. I am sorry to make it sound so simple. Actually, it is not simple, for better schools depend on better public understanding. I do not believe I could get up in a public school board meeting anywhere in the country and talk about these problems and get a hearing of any consequence. I do not believe I would expect any real sympathy from the group as a whole. After the meeting, people would come up and say, "I was interested in what you had to say," and that would be that.

For the community at large, there just wouldn't be much interest. A typical suburban community today is having its troubles with a rejected school budget every other year, protests against reading teachers, protests against libraries, and protests against everything you think of that raises educational levels. There is pretty clear evidence that the knowledge of the problem is not distributed as we would like. This is why I made the earlier suggestion that we dramatize our problem as a national problem through the instrument of some kind of a national, truly public, foundation.

All of us here worry about our role. I think we worry with justification. The thought that struck me again and again both yesterday and this morning is that what people were demanding, as they spoke, was devotion and personal service. Perhaps we should become angry men in the sense suggested by Gerald Green's fine book *The Last Angry Man*. Perhaps one of the real solutions to our problem is that there should be one angry man about talent.

Conference Participants

Lucile Allen, Consultant, Austin College, Sherman, Texas

Homer D. Babbidge, Jr., Assistant Commissioner for Higher Education, Office of Education, Department of Health, Education, and Welfare, Washington 25, D.C.

Ralph F. Berdie, Professor of Psychology and Director of Student Counseling Bureau, University of Minnesota, Minneapolis 14, Minnesota

Horace Mann Bond, Dean, School of Education, Atlanta University, Atlanta, Georgia

Frank H. Bowles, President, College Entrance Examination Board, 475 Riverside Drive, New York 27, N.Y.

Justin W. Brierly, Coordinator, College and Scholarship Counseling, Denver Public Schools, Denver 2, Colorado

Roy C. Buck, Associate Professor of Rural Sociology, College of Agriculture, Pennsylvania State University, University Park, Pennsylvania

Frederick C. Copeland, Director of Admissions, Williams College, Williamstown, Massachusetts

John G. Darley, Executive Secretary, American Psychological Association, 1333 Sixteenth Street, N.W., Washington 6, D.C.

Alex A. Daughtry, Chairman, Division of Teacher Education, Kansas State Teachers College, Emporia, Kansas

A. Luini del Russo, General Attorney, Public Education Section, Commission on Civil Rights, Washington 25, D.C.

Lawrence E. Dennis, Vice-President for Academic Affairs, Pennsylvania State University, University Park, Pennsylvania

Mrs. Jane Lee J. Eddy, Executive Secretary, Taconic Foundation, Inc., 666 Fifth Avenue, New York 19, N.Y.

Warren G. Findley, Assistant Superintendent for Pupil Personnel Services, Board of Education of the City of Atlanta, Atlanta, Georgia

D. H. Gardner, Vice-President and Dean of Administration, University of Akron, Akron 4, Ohio

Frederick Garrigus, Manager of Organizational Services, National Association of Broadcasters, 1771 N Street, N.W., Washington 6, D.C.

Carl F. Hansen, Superintendent of Schools of the District of Columbia, Washington 5, D.C.

Melvene D. Hardee, Professor, School of Education, Florida State University, Tallahassee, Florida

Robert J. Havighurst, Professor of Education, Committee on Human Development, University of Chicago, Chicago 37, Illinois

Algo D. Henderson, Director, Center for the Study of Higher Education, University of Michigan, Ann Arbor, Michigan

Mrs. A. L. Hendrick, Vice-President, Region VI, National Congress of Parents and Teachers, 504 Road of Remembrance, Jackson, Mississippi

Raymond C. Hummel, Assistant Professor of Education, Graduate School of Education, Harvard University, Cambridge 38, Massachusetts

Robert E. Iffert, Chief, Faculty and Student Services, Office of Education, Department of Health, Education, and Welfare, Washington 25, D.C.

Frederick H. Jackson, Executive Associate, Carnegie Corporation of New York, 589 Fifth Avenue, New York 17, N.Y.

Samuel W. Jacobs, Assistant Superintendent, Westmoreland County Public Schools, Greensburg, Pennsylvania

J. Kenneth Little, Associate Director, Committee on Institutional Cooperation, University of Wisconsin, Madison, Wisconsin

Ray C. Maul, Assistant Director, Research Division, National Education Association, 1201 Sixteenth Street, N.W., Washington 6, D.C.

John U. Monro, Dean, Harvard College, Cambridge 38, Massachusetts

Rexford G. Moon, Jr., Director of the College Scholarship Service, College Entrance Examination Board, 475 Riverside Drive, New York 27, N.Y.

Glyn Morris, Assistant Superintendent in Charge of Pupil Personnel, Lewis County, Lyons Falls, New York

George E. Mowrer, Director of Guidance, Board of Education of the City of St. Louis, St. Louis 1, Missouri

Florence C. Myers, Administrative Assistant in Charge of Guidance, George Washington High School, 549 Audubon Avenue, New York 40, N.Y.

Elizabeth Paschal, Associate Program Director, Education Division, The Ford Foundation, 477 Madison Avenue, New York 22, N.Y.

Richard L. Plaut, President, National Scholarship Service and Fund for Negro Students, 6 East 82nd Street, New York 28, N.Y.

Alice M. Rivlin, Research Assistant, The Brookings Institution, Washington 6, D.C.

Mrs. Nellie Rosebaugh, Director of College Guidance, Glenville High School, Cleveland, Ohio

Daniel Schreiber, Coordinator, Higher Horizons Program, Board of Education of the City of New York, Brooklyn 1, New York

David Shulman, Counselor, George Washington High School, 549 Audubon Avenue, New York 40, N.Y.

Sister Ann Francis, S.N.D., Dean of Students, Trinity College, Washington, D.C.

Sister Columba, S.N.D., Academic Vice-President, Trinity College, Washington, D.C.

Sister Margaret, S.N.D., President, Trinity College, Washington, D.C.

Rev. Andrew C. Smith, S.J., President, Spring Hill College, Mobile, Alabama

Lyman J. Smith, Executive Director, Illinois State Scholarship Commission, Deerfield, Illinois

John M. Stalnaker, President, National Merit Scholarship Corporation, 1580 Sherman Avenue, Evanston, Illinois

Glen Stice, Research Associate, Educational Testing Service, 20 Nassau Street, Princeton, New Jersey

Francis Stroup, Associate Professor of Physical Education, Northern Illinois University, De Kalb, Illinois

Donald E. Super, Professor of Education, Teachers College, Columbia University, New York 27, N.Y.

Ann Tanneyhill, Director of Vocational Services, National Urban League, Inc., 14 East 48th Street, New York 17, N.Y.

John J. Theobald, Superintendent of Schools, Board of Education of the City of New York, Brooklyn 1, New York

A. F. Tuttle, Director of Admissions, Stetson University, DeLand, Florida

Clyde Vroman, Director of Admissions, University of Michigan, Ann Arbor, Michigan

Dael Wolfle, Executive Director, American Association for the Advancement of Science, 1515 Massachusetts Avenue, N.W., Washington 5, D.C.

Herbert L. Wright, Youth Secretary, National Association for the Advancement of Colored People, 20 West 40th Street, New York 18, N.Y.

Wendell W. Wright, Professor of Education, Indiana University, Bloomington, Indiana

Arthur S. Adams, President, American Council on Education

Nicholas C. Brown, Staff Associate, American Council on Education

AMERICAN COUNCIL ON EDUCATION

Arthur S. Adams, *President*

The American Council on Education is a *council* of national associations; organizations having related interests; approved universities, colleges, teachers colleges, junior colleges, technological schools, and selected private secondary schools; state departments of education; city school systems and private school systems; selected educational departments of business and industrial companies; voluntary associations of higher education in the states; and large public libraries. It is a center of cooperation and coordination whose influence has been apparent in the shaping of American educational policies and the formation of educational practices during the past forty-two years.

PB6-13
J